PSYCHIC SENSE

Other titles by Mary Swainson:

The Spirit of Counsel

With Ruth White:
Gildas Communicates
Seven Inner Journeys
The Healing Spectrum

Mary Swainson, MA, DPhil, was instrumental in building a counselling service for university students in the 1950s to early 1970s. Jungian psychology and psychotherapy have formed the main background to her work, leading to investigations in the area of psychic awareness and the states of consciousness associated with it. She has worked with many psychics, helping them to develop their abilities and making known her findings through various books and journals.

Louisa Bennett, BSc, took her degree in psychology as a mature student. She has brought up three children, two boys and one girl, now grown up. She has trained and worked with the Samaritans, and taken part in a student counselling service. Her interests include outdoor activities and a love for animals.

PSYCHIC SENSE
Training and Developing Psychic Sensitivity

Mary Swainson & Louisa Bennett

1990
Llewellyn Publications
St. Paul, Minnesota 55164-0383, U.S.A.

Q quantum © W. Foulsham & Co. Ltd.

First U.S. Edition, 1990
First Printing, 1990

Cover art by Tom Canny

Library of Congress Cataloging-in-Publication Data

Swainson, Mary.
    Psychic sense: training and developing psychic sensitivity /
by Mary Swainson & Louisa Bennett.
     p.   cm.
    Includes bibliographical references and index.
    ISBN 0-87542-771-5
    1. Parapsychology. 2. Psychic ability. 3. Psychics.
I. Bennett, Louisa. II. Title.
BF 1031.S95 1990   90-48832
133.8—dc20   CIP

This Llewellyn/Quantum edition produced for
U.S.A. and Canada under license by:

Llewellyn Publications
A Division of Llewellyn Worldwide, Ltd.
P.O. Box 64383, St. Paul, MN 55164-0383, U.S.A.

And I have felt
A presence that disturbs me with the joy
Of elevated thought; a sense sublime
Of something far more deeply interfused,
Whose dwelling is the light of setting suns,
And the round ocean and the living air,
And the blue sky and in the mind of man:
A motion and a spirit, that impels
All thinking things, all objects of all thought,
And rolls through all things.

Wordsworth: *Tintern Abbey*

From Louisa
   For 'Pops'
   The man who gave me free integrity

From Mary
   For Nabraham and his group
   With thanks and love

CONTENTS

Preface   10

PART ONE   INTRODUCTION   13

CHAPTER 1   15

   MARY'S STORY
   Early Years
   Outer Work: Psychology and Counselling
   Inner Development: The White Eagle Lodge
   'The World behind the World': K
   Ruth White and the Work with Gildas

CHAPTER 2   34

   NEW DIMENSIONS IN COUNSELLING
   AND PSYCHOTHERAPY
   Levels in Psychotherapy
   The Ego and the Self
   The Shadow

CHAPTER 3   46

   EXPLORING INNER WORLDS
   An Historical Perspective
   A Practical Present-day Approach to Other
   Worlds

The Need for Education of the Psychic
Faculties

Preparation for Mediumship

PART TWO   A LIFE ON THE PATH   63

CHAPTER 4   65

LOUISA'S STORY

From the Beginning, *by Louisa*
Preparation and Training, *by Mary*
Further Tests and Achievements
An Experiment

CHAPTER 5   78

THE EXERCISES

Early Stages: Guides and Systems of Guidance
The Psychic Levels: Problems encountered in
Spontaneous Psychic Development
Past Lives and Reincarnation
Group Souls
Time
The Nature of Soul

CHAPTER 6   127

AN EVALUATION

A Critique of Channelling, *by Jessica and Louisa*
Afterword, *by Mary*
Comment from a Discarnate Guide,
by Nabraham
Conclusion, *by Nabraham*

Glossary   142

Suggestions for Further Reading   146

Appendix: Mediumship and the Christian Churches   150

Index   159

ACKNOWLEDGEMENTS

We thank Jessica for taking part in the experiment, Hazel Marshall for typing, and the questioners for their help in evoking the answers received and in providing valuable practice for the sensitives.

We are grateful to the editor of *Light*, Brenda Marshall, for her encouragement in the early stages, her advice on the reading list, and permission to use several papers. Acknowledgements are also due to Johan Quanjer, editor of the journal *New Humanity*, for allowing us to include articles and for his stimulating challenges. Lastly we thank Bill Anderton, former editor of *Soluna*, not only for permission to reprint material from that journal but especially now, as our present editor, for his perceptive suggestions and care in the preparation of this book.

The terms 'Brothers' and 'Brotherhood' are used in the script, just as Nabraham gave them, but with no sexist connotation. To write 'Brotherhood/Sisterhood' or 'Brothers and Sisters' every time, although true, would have been clumsy. In the more subtle worlds gender becomes less significant, especially when the concept of reincarnation — sometimes as male sometimes as female — is taken into account.

PREFACE

Why did we write this book? Through our work together it has been growing spontaneously for the last ten or twelve years. From time to time different aspects have been published as articles in specialist journals, but their readership is limited and we feel that now the time has come to present it to the general public.

Our main aim is to show the need for both recognition and education of the psychic faculties, especially in the case of potential sensitives or 'mediums'. These are individuals who are able to 'mediate' between the personal and transpersonal levels of being, and who are therefore of great value to our suffering, materialistic world *if* soundly prepared. In particular we stress the importance of both psychological and experiential preparation of the personality before perception and transmission of good quality can be achieved.

In the introductory Part One, Mary, not a medium herself, describes how, throughout her life, she was progressively led to work with sensitives in the early stages of their development. She soon found that levels in psychotherapy needed to be extended in order to include further dimensions. Some problematic, practical and theoretical issues arising out of such transpersonal work are then examined.

In Part Two, Louisa, a medium then in training, describes the path of development from her point of view. This is the main part of our contribution, comprising the accurate detailed records of exercises and teachings received, combined with some critical evaluation. We hope that the content and varying levels of answers to questions may form a basis for discussion.

Those researching into the nature of mediumship may find these records particularly interesting — perhaps unique — in that Louisa shares the same inner source as her sister Jessica; in fact it was Jessica who first found Nabraham on an inner journey. This has led to a useful experiment, described fully in the text, when the same question receives answers separately from the two sisters.

As to the source, Nabraham (pronounced 'Narbraham') tells us that he belongs to a teaching group of Brothers in the discarnate planes of existence. For readers who may be somewhat sceptical about this statement, names are used only for convenience. Who he is, or was when in incarnation, is not important. The true teaching guides do not wish to be judged by names or reputation but simply by the quality of their work. If some of it should 'ring a bell' for you that is enough. So we present this book for readers' thoughtful assessment.

PART ONE

INTRODUCTION

In all forms, both outer and inner, the twentieth century is a time of turmoil and change. Many people find that it is sufficient to choose to remain fixed and let these changes pass them by. But for those to whom this would mean a living death, it is necessary to live a constantly dying life — letting go the outworn, opening up the new. Space exploration, for example, refers not only to the outer universe but also to inner space/time. Frightening? It may be so; yet there is always the thrill of a great adventure, infinitely meaningful and infinitely rewarding.

Remaining true to one's own nature and field of being can allow the discovery of the unique, individual way that is our own essential part to play in the cosmos: the bit, however small, that no one else can do. Although stepping out of collective customs and stereotypes may feel at first lonely, the individual way does not necessarily imply that one is alone. Far from it; one is magnetically drawn to connect with others who are also finding themselves, and so we come to work in pairs, small groups and wider networks. The test is to relate to one another not as partial units of a herd but as increasingly fulfilled beings. A further check tells us that at each stage somehow it 'feels right'. Certainly our perception of truth and of purpose may alter and deepen as we travel but at any one moment it should ring true; we should recognise it. This will be true no matter how hard the way or how confused our conscious minds may be, especially during periods of rapid change. With the aging process comes the ability to see more and more of the pattern that lies behind, marvelling at the significance and beauty of every aspect of it, dark or light. Therefore, now

13

that I have reached the age of eighty-one, perhaps my best contribution in introducing Louisa's distinctive path is first to share my own way through this troubled yet vitally important century. At the outset, however, I should make it clear that I myself am not a medium, nor am I psychic but I have considerable experience in working with those who are.

CHAPTER 1
MARY'S STORY

Early Years — Outer Work: Psychology and Counselling —
Inner Development: The White Eagle Lodge — 'The World
Behind the World' — Ruth White and the Work with Gildas

EARLY YEARS

As a country child I was something of a nature mystic, passionately seeking loving communion with animals, trees, and the sea, yet intuitively aware of 'something far more deeply interfused'. When seventeen, at boarding school, I had a near-death experience which was so intensely real in its heightened livingness that I have never been afraid to die; this incarnate life is far more alarming. Like many in their teens and early twenties, I wrote verse, finding that dimly perceived truths could best come into consciousness through my pen. Thus, in an immature way, I discovered the door of the arts: how to make contact with the hidden source of wisdom by poetic imagination. Through writing and to some extent music I became aware of other states of consciousness: of pre-existence and of more heightened, more beautiful, conditions of being. Poetry came so easily that it felt strangely ready-made, as though I had trodden this way before. (At school I could tell stories to the dormitory without effort — they just flowed — and later I wrote them.) Yet while I respect and in some ways regret the path of inspiration through one form of the arts, I knew

15

deep down that in this present day of life a different, harder work was to be done.

At university, although I wrote for, then edited the students' magazine, my critical mind began to take over, particularly since I was reading a more earthy and scientific subject — geography — in which I took my first two degrees, and then taught it for some years. Researching in rural settlements in the beautiful south west of England was a joyous love affair with the land: good in that it helped to integrate heart and mind, art and science. But there was a price to pay. Many of us, leaving the magical awareness of childhood and youth, must go through the darkness and confusion of the intellectual/critical period, questioning everything. My understanding father, who had been through it himself, called this the 'ten years chaos phase', and indeed for me it lasted about that time, from eighteen to twenty eight. It was valuable in that I hope to have retained and developed a degree of objective and questioning open-mindedness about these elusive, intuitive intimations and phenomena. At the same time I plunged into the outer world of work (teaching in colleges and universities) and later the experiences of love and war — a period of intense living, wonderful, terrible, and often painful — yet value and meaning are found more in the market place than in dreams. And, of the three ultimate values, beauty, truth and goodness, although beauty infused my early life, and goodness tended to be culturally imposed in a not altogether healthy way, my chosen path this time round has always been truth. Like Kipling's mongoose Rikki Tikki Tavi, a main incentive for living is 'Run and find out'. Astrologically, my Sun symbol, representing the higher self bringing its main purpose into this incarnation, is in the fiery, pioneering sign of Aries. But the Sun has to shine through the 'lens' of the present personality which for me is in the sensitive, watery sign of Cancer. Fire and water do not mix, so pioneering has often been painful. Further, Saturn conjunct Sun has brought limitation, discipline, plenty of hard work and earthing of ideas. And so there had to be a shift from poetry and fiction writing to research in a more documentary mode: from love of nature and animals (the 'unfallen' world as my father called it) to work with people. Life has been a series of constant deaths and re-births.

OUTER WORK: PSYCHOLOGY AND COUNSELLING

After some years of geographic research and teaching I found the subject dying on me. As a tutor in a teacher training college I became interested in education and child guidance in particular. Research turned to investigation, first into children's preferences in geography, then in religious education, followed by a fascinating study of their concepts of God (crucial for all later therapy with adults). Published in *Religion in Education*, this led to two years, before and after the war, spent at Oxford reading for a D. Phil. in educational psychology, the subject of my thesis being *The Moral Ideas of Children and Adolescents*.

Child guidance was then in its early stages in Britain, but while teaching at a university during and after the war, I trained at the local clinic, then enriched by immigrant psychiatrists from Germany and Austria. I specialised in play therapy — much needed for evacuees — and have since found this of immense value in working with the child in people of all ages. It soon became clear that an essential part of training was work on oneself, so I began a personal analysis which was to last for ten years off and on. It involved four analysts, two men and two women: the founder of the Group-Analytic School, a Freudian, and two Jungians. (Jungian psychology has always been my main theoretical background, but I am glad of the experience of other schools.) Near its inauguration I became a member of the group that was to become the British Association of

Psychotherapists, training as far as was then possible to become a psychotherapist and counsellor. The history of building a pioneer counselling service for university students from the 1950s to the early 1970s is told in detail in my autobiography, as well as much more of my personal life.[1] On one level this service, its extension to other colleges in the area, to tutors and (mainly after retirement) to private individuals of all ages, turned out to be the main outer life task this time round.

INNER DEVELOPMENT: THE WHITE EAGLE LODGE

On another level, and running parallel, was my inner life. Although as an Anglican clergyman's daughter I was brought up with a sound religious grounding, I soon began to rebel at the limitations (as I saw them) of the orthodox church and, especially during that 'ten years chaos' period, began to look further afield. In my twenties and early thirties I read a good deal of other, mainly Eastern, religions and philosophies, especially those that drew from the Ageless Wisdom which rang a bell for me.

One such source was Lawrence Hyde's excellent correspondence course in 'Spiritual Science'; I tried many groups and cults; for four years I was even in Subud which certainly helped to put me in touch with my body but taught me to beware of opening up schizophrenics! However, when I found the White Eagle Lodge I felt I had come home. The teaching was simple yet pure, with subtle depths, directed mainly at developing the heart centre, which I needed. And I was fortunate to find and belong to the Lodge during the heyday of Grace Cooke's (Minesta's) work as a medium

---

1. Mary Swainson, *The Spirit of Counsel*, Spearman, 1977. Now published by The C.W. Daniel Co. Ltd.

when in small groups we received regular individual messages and invaluable personal guidance directly from White Eagle. I joined before the war started, but when their country home was established[2] I was able to attend annual retreats for over twenty years (1946 to 1966), carrying me through that difficult middle period of life from thirty-eight to fifty-eight. Indeed, for fifty-one weeks in the year I felt like a ship at sea, at last able to go for one week into harbour for a blessed refit. I don't know how I would have survived without those retreats. But, as ever on the path, we all found that if much is given, much is demanded; the spiritual education we received was to be tested out more and more stringently in the outer world in the intervening period. Yet this is how we grow.

In the early years, before I had any conscious idea of what my work was to be, like the others I was given the sense of a distinct mission to be accomplished, yet always assured that 'You will have the help equivalent'. Depending always on my free will, I could be an instrument for the Brotherhood in writing, speaking, and work with the young. Of course, at the time I took all this with a considerable pinch of salt; my mind was sceptical, my emotions rebellious. But rebellion and doubt were invariably met by complete respect for choice, by calm acceptance, gentle humour and wise answers, displacing the apparent conflict to a deeper level of understanding.

Personal guidance in the early years monitored my steady though slow development. How thankful I am now that it was able to be spread over so many years contrasted with the sudden, sometimes almost violent opening up which so many seem to experience as the century draws to its close. Once White Eagle teased me gently for being 'Mary the Mind' whereas another group member was 'Mary the Heart'. I needed to develop feeling and was advised always

---

2. The White Eagle Lodge, New Lands, Rake, Liss, Hampshire GU33 7HY.

to seek tranquillity, something I have not found easy. When I began counselling he warned me against over-enthusiasm. 'Do not try to carry the karma of others . . .[3] Do not force a soul to go the way you want it to go . . . Hold it in the light and give sympathy and love . . . Surrender all to God.' And for my own (then turbulent) life, 'Do not resent karma; you are like a lion in a net; cut loose the strings that bind.' Again, 'Heights and depths are equally part of God.'

In this work the centres or chakras in the subtle body are stimulated and harmonised (see Glossary). Each centre represents different attributes and functions. When in 1953 I was initiated into the Inner Brotherhood, particular reference was made to my crown and heart centres representing respectively intuition and feeling. (Note: not thought!) After that, the insights became much deeper, coming less through teaching, more through my own meditation, for during the retreats we were all trained in meditation and given teaching of a general as well as a personal kind. Most of us had already served an apprenticeship in distant healing, and those who lived sufficiently near to New Lands or to the London Lodge were able to practise contact healing as well. Each in our different ways was preparing for suitable service.

Where the specific theme of this book is concerned, I cannot be too grateful for the experience of receiving all this valuable training through a first class medium. It gave me a standard by which to assess others. Minesta was always genuinely humble and self-critical about her work. White Eagle himself would urge us never to take his words without discrimination, always to test them against the insight of our own deepest being. Such an attitude not only increased trust but also strengthened our reliance on our own sources.

---

3. In this context White Eagle was referring to the redemptive purpose and task for which we incarnated. Each individual must be responsible for his or her own karma. For a fuller definition see Glossary.

Through meditation we were progressively introduced to this inner knower and in many cases also to our guides. Unlike the domination of some gurus, true independence was encouraged: 'Follow your own star'. So my questioning mind was increasingly satisfied. Indeed, this twenty-year period of spiritual education, based on the Ageless Wisdom, paralleled the more orthodox psychological analysis, never conflicting but complementary. Further, White Eagle was open to contact with other groups and teachers, in fact he would send messages of love and brotherhood when I went on straight from New Lands to see Lawrence Hyde.[4] It was important to me that freedom was respected. I was told, 'We would not hamper you in any way.' On the other hand, in the idiom of his American Indian incarnation — this was only one of his 'dresses' for a very great soul lay behind the name — he used to advise us, once having found the path that felt right, to stick to it and go deeply into it. 'Do not make squirrel tracks.'

I can never appreciate sufficiently the effect that White Eagle, Minesta, and all the family had on my subsequent life and work. It was at the Lodge that I met many lifelong 'friends of the spirit' as one of them termed it, including, at one of the earlier retreats, Paul Beard and his wife Rosemary. Later, Paul was to be the President of the College of Psychic Studies[5] of which I soon became a member, gave several talks, and have been a regular contributor to their journal, *Light*. Here is one of the best sources for the study of psychic and spiritual matters, with the largest special

---

4. Lawrence Hyde (1896–1958), a one-time editor of *Light* (journal of the College of Psychic Studies), published seven books on spiritual philosophy, one of which I reviewed. It has been said by his literary executor, Charlotte Waterlow, that in the Platonic tradition, 'He was trying to express in intellectual terms the insights gained from initiation into the sacred mysteries. His books have so far had little impact perhaps because their message belongs to the 21st century.'

5. The College of Psychic Studies, 16 Queensberry Place, London SW7 2EB.

library of its kind in the country. Particularly it is a sound resource for investigating mediumship, offering as it does courses of training, lectures, workshops, sessions with first-class sensitives, healing, and individual help and guidance, particularly for bereavement.

In these and other ways I found inner support and back-up for my outer work. Of course I could not introduce what I had learned directly into teaching and counselling except to a very, very few. For even what is now orthodox counselling was then hardly acceptable to academics; medicals particularly were at first exceptionally resistant, one elderly doctor calling what I was doing 'witchcraft'. However, the inner experience permeated my relationships with students. And not only students; as the counselling work developed, tutors requested groups to discuss student problems, inevitably leading on to their own difficulties in handling students, and from there, in a few cases, to training in tutorial work involving some personal psychotherapy. They came both from the university and from other colleges in the area. It was through one of these tutors that I first made direct contact with the amazing inner world of another person.

'THE WORLD BEHIND THE WORLD': K

K, a tutor in a teacher training college (now called a college of education) was a little older than I. Although inwardly diffident, outwardly she was a powerful personality, original and able. Her students and colleagues both loved and feared her yet deeply respected her standard of work with them.

Looking back now, I can see that she presented me with one of the most frightening yet creative challenges I have ever met. It was one thing to have read (mainly in Jung) about these phenomena, or to have experienced their inner images during guided meditation in the safety of a retreat. It was quite another to encounter them in reality in a human being for whom I was responsible in so far as I was her therapist. Inexperienced as I was then (in my middle forties) I made some bad mistakes. I became far too emotionally involved. I realised that I had taken on more than I could handle, especially since I was forbidden by confidentiality to discuss the matter with our consultant psychiatrist. At one time, when I had unwittingly let her down, I felt like Judas, one of the worst pains I have ever known. However, even that had to be accepted and later, through private help and healing for myself from the Lodge, I was able to become more detached. There I was told that it was a deep, karmic relationship, to be resolved if possible in this life. That helped. I have found since that karmic involvements, though infinitely worth while if they can be redeemed, cause far more difficulty than if the karmic factor is absent.

K had already undergone some analysis, but she both wanted and needed to plumb depths so far untried by either of us. So it was a journey of discovery where possibly my interest and her inner drive overcame our caution. She had always suffered periods of deep depression, but through her own strength had found a way to come out of them. One of her chief anxieties was that any person who encountered her true inner state would not be strong enough to take the impact, and would die on her. Apparently this had happened a few times, including the recent death of her analyst, though I do not suppose for that reason. Therefore, one thing I determined: that however ill I might be (and I did become fairly ill at the change of life involving a major operation) I would not do that to her again. At one period a temporary separation was necessary while we both regained stability on our own. And in the end we won through. I stress all this to show the dangers for those who are, as I then was, relatively inexperienced. Yet with hindsight I can see now that it all had to happen.

K was essentially an artist although when we first met her

paintings were somewhat inhibited. To add to the difficulty, in temperament she was my complete opposite. In his theory of psychological types, apart from the well-known attitude types of introversion and extraversion, Jung recognised four main functions: thinking, feeling, sensation and intuition. People with naturally strong and developed thinking tend to be weak in feeling, and vice versa, similarly with the other pair of opposite functions, sensation and intuition. K's strongest function was sensation, with feeling secondary, whereas I am mainly an intuitive type with trained thinking. Although hampering communication, our complementary natures were potentially enriching to us both. I had already met a similar pattern with one of my analysts, a sensation type who did not understand, yet valued, my intuitive side. After some standard reductive therapy dealing with her childhood, K asked me to teach her to meditate. This I did joyfully, with no thought for what it might open up, although later I realised I might have been warned since her early years had shown a distinctly withdrawn and isolated pattern.

Characteristically, she found her own way into meditation quite differently from the way in which I had been trained. Immediately she was deep in an inner world where, she later confessed, she had always lived; in many ways it was more real to her than the outer. In my own analysis, of course, I had considerable experience of appropriate archetypal symbols emerging through dreams, imaging, and meditation, but to me these never had the overwhelming reality that K's inner world had for her. At the time I hardly knew what we were going into; it was certainly a major learning process for us both. The lesson for my future work was to use greater caution.

Looking back, I can now see the early indications. In her first meditation (typically concentrating on an *actual* outer golden flower — brown-eyed Susan — not an inner image) the flower 'told' her, 'The light and the dark are two halves. If you go into the dark you will find the light and be born again. Out of the dark comes light.' She plunged straight into an inner journey where, for forty days during which I could do nothing except be with her, she sat in deep depression in a cave 'in the centre of the earth' until the time was right for her to come out 'by a new and living way'. In such journeys, universal symbols and images tend to well up from the collective unconscious of the race; in K's case these archetypes (see Glossary) appeared to her in living actuality. They included the dragon guarding the well of living water, the primaeval toad, and many, many others; I remember particularly the sacrificial hare leading to a crucifixion experience in which her too-strong ego-personality was reduced to the size of a pea. Above all was the snake, sacred libido symbol which, passing through all the classical transformations within her body, was finally redeemed and raised to the crown centre. The well known caterpillar/chrysalis/butterfly transition ran parallel. Yet throughout, I was relieved to find, were consistent, positive symbols of the Self — the deep centre beyond the ego — starting with a still, circular pool containing a central island in the middle of which stood a single tree. In the trunk of this great oak she was reborn. The tree then followed her throughout her journey up a steep valley, providing nourishment from its roots. Finally she reached the holy mountain, a scene which she often painted.

I did my best, reading all the sources I could find in order to comprehend and offer possible interpretations of what was going on, but in general I could do little except be there, alongside.

In many people's inner journeys which I have monitored since, the guides or inner teachers have been there from the beginning. This is an immense help to all concerned, since they can explain so much that is beyond our limited three-dimensional vision. But in K's case the guide did not appear until near the end. Perhaps again this was characteristic, for the artist in her deeply distrusted words or logical thought, seeing only their abuse. Yet, to balance up her personality, she needed just what she despised: to build and relate to the male 'animus' aspect of her psyche and the 'logos' principle in a positive way. However, when most of the suffering was over, she found her guide in a beautiful inner landscape full of flowers. Here, gently and slowly he put into simple concepts and meaning all that she had lived through, consolidating and explaining the gruelling yet wonderful experiences. In particular he helped her to link the two worlds, inner and outer, and to come back, more fully reborn as a person, into her daily life and work. But the return was hard. Like so many gifted souls who have been there she felt different afterwards. In her journey diary she wrote, 'I can see the Mountain of God and I could cry my eyes out because I am here and not there. I do not belong here. I am an exile.' The guide comforted, 'But so often you forget that you have an uncommon gift: you can see the world behind the world. Many people would give a great deal for this gift. Mary envies it. You often envy her greater certainty about life. But this is your certainty, your gift. Hold on to it.' She did.

K never expressed her insights in any form of mediumship, but for the following twenty-three years until her death she was able to integrate them into her relationships and her many creative outer activities in a way that she could not do before. During this period naturally I saw much less of her, since our true work was completed, but we remained friends. After retirement she travelled abroad; I well remember a vivid painting which captured the restless, volcanic, new-earth landscape of Jamaica. Even towards the end, her constant cry was 'Life — more life!' Shortly before she died, I visited her frequently in the nursing home, telling her of my own near-death experience and reminding her of the mountain and the glorious valley of flowers in her inner world where her wise and loving guide would be waiting. For, although on a redemptive journey there can be much darkness, there are also great beauty and intense joy. As her golden flower had told her right at the outset, 'Out of the dark comes light.' Throughout a long illness she showed immense courage and never lost her sense of humour, but by that time the inner realities had become relatively distant from her waking consciousness. It is not easy to keep in touch when the body is weak with discomfort and great pain.

As an artist, shunning words, K hated to write letters. However, looking through her papers I have discovered a note to me, scribbled on the inside of an old envelope a few years after the therapy had been completed. At least it showed that we had both learned to respect our opposite natures. She had written, 'I found your letter interesting because I don't think in this way. I'm not aware. I just paint. Also I found it encouraging and permissive, letting me be myself and finding value in it. You realise, don't you, that I would never have had the courage without the work we did together and are still doing? Do you remember the dead, frightened little paintings I used to do? So, thank you, Mary.'

'The work we are still doing.' Towards the end of, and after her therapy, I helped to train her in counselling, and for some years she helped me in the student service by running an art therapy group and training others to run them. In this and in her tutorial work with her own students she was able to bring through the values of self-discovery, so that those who had problems were less alarmed at being referred to our service. It was in this way that I met her student Ruth White. And I thank *you*, K, for everything.

This descripion of my first initiation into deep inner work has been given in some detail, partly because (unlike Ruth's) it has never been published before, although it could well make a book on its own; partly because I realise how much it taught me. Sometimes I was anxious and frightened. Less so when she had out-of-the-body trips on a psychic level, for these I understood to some extent, though I did not encourage them. But I shall never forget the time when psychological trauma temporarily reversed red and green traffic lights in K's brain. A journey of some distance to a work commitment was unavoidable. I do not drive myself, but I had a strong hunch to go with her, sensing that her unconscious mind would not endanger my life, since I was, at the time, too important to her; otherwise her own life might have been in danger, let alone those of others. Throughout, I was always protected and given inner guidance, never tried quite beyond my strength. So I learned to trust.

What else? I learned not to be afraid of psychological darkness, in the Jungian sense of the Shadow, for in it, as he has shown us, lies the gold. Heaven knows there were many lessons by trial and error, chiefly error, but I learned to accept and forgive myself, for if I did the best I could at the time, no one can do more. A maxim practised ever since, and passed on to those I have trained and supervised, is, 'Whatever happens, use it.' Above all, I learned to see each person as a totally specific individual climbing his or her own unique route up the side of the holy mountain, and to respect their variants of the major archetypal symbols. Of great importance was the recognition of the need to find and accept the help of the inner guide as early on the journey as possible.

Therefore, by the time I came to work in depth with Ruth and later with others (men and women, though most were women) I had more experience to fall back on, more confidence to trust the process. With Ruth we plumbed even deeper levels, but this time — especially as she was so much younger than K — I remembered the need for caution, for we both have Sun in Aries, and Ariens tend to rush in. Early in Ruth's work, when she was discussing with her inner guide, Gildas, her relationship with me, he said, 'Mary is somewhat over-cautious with you. She has rather too much respect for the fact that you tend to be so sensitive. I sometimes get the impression that she is afraid to hurt you.' True indeed, after my experience with K, and possibly an over-reaction?

RUTH WHITE AND THE WORK WITH GILDAS

If establishing a student counselling service was the main outer, more conventional task in this day of life, relationship with Ruth and her inner guide and teacher, Gildas, has certainly been my peak experience and most rewarding venture on psychic and spiritual levels. For about twenty-four years, from the mid 1950s to around 1980, we worked together in great harmony. Then Ruth rightly began to pioneer her own pattern of service. Now she has an established, busy practice in England and Europe. She works with counselling and guidance in cooperation with Gildas and leads a number of workshops. Part of each year she spends writing in Provence.[6] From small beginnings her work has grown beyond all recognition, and I feel privileged to have taken part in the early stages.

At the age of nineteen, Ruth was referred to the student counselling service by her tutor K. Because of long-standing eye trouble (indeed she had been told she might become blind) she suffered from understandable depression. It soon became evident that she was exceptionally gifted psychically in a way totally unrecognised by her family and by our materialistic culture generally (although fortunately, in view of her own experience, K had an inkling of it). As Dr Arthur Guirdham has so often suggested, psychic abilities, if repressed and unrecognised, can lie at the root of many so-called psychosomatic illnesses, and it is interesting to note that during the first year or two of our work, Ruth's eyesight stabilised. My first aim, therefore, was recognition.

---

6. Address in England: Black Bear Flat, 57 Oakhurst Grove, East Dulwich, London SE22 9AH.

Address in France: Le Petit Canadeau, Le Plan du Castellet, 83330 Le Beausset, France.

I lent her books by Joan Grant, particularly *Winged Pharaoh*, to give her some sense of companionship, of being less isolated in her inner vision. At that early date these were all I could find describing psychic perception, since for reasons of confidentiality I could not speak of K's inner world with her own student, nor have I done so until now.

Our work began with normal counselling, but soon Ruth went into an inner journey where, fortunately for us both, her inner guide appeared almost at once, with no suggestion from me. So we had his help throughout a total of seven journeys, each more testing and gruelling than the last, but including periods of great beauty, joy and achievement. Together with the here-and-now psychological work that they mirrored, these journeys formed Ruth's personal and transpersonal preparation over the first twelve years from 1956 to 1968. The full story is told in the second book that we published.[7]

Later, Ruth relived some relevant aspects of many past lives. These effected deeper personal clearance and also had much wider significance for, as Gildas often told us, all we do for ourselves is inevitably done for all humanity, 'mirrored and magnified on every level'. As yet these are unpublished, but the experience has enabled her to work in this field now with others. Here we were exploring hitherto 'uncharted territory' as Gildas termed it. At times it was quite alarming for us both but, thank heaven, we had Gildas' wise guidance throughout. For only the true inner guide can monitor the right timing, pace, degree of challenge, and depth of such crucial work. I shall never cease to be astonished at Ruth's constant, brave persistence through all those years. At the time it was severely demanding, often painful, but later she knew the experiences to be infinitely worth while; never would she have wished to go back and leave them undone.

---

7. Ruth White and Mary Swainson, *Seven Inner Journeys*, Spearman, 1974. Now published by The C.W. Daniel Company.

What is achieved personally cannot help but emanate to others. To start with Ruth was so aware of Gildas' presence that we three could sometimes hold conversations. Then he began to answer questions from friends, and soon this led to personal and general teachings. He always preferred the question and answer method, recognising the spiritual law that the incentive must come from us; as Christ said, 'Ask and ye shall receive.' Beginning in a small way, we issued these teachings by post twice or three times a year to interested people. This 'Readers' Group' produced still more questions which kept us busy. At its maximum the group numbered over 700, so that when the books began to be published Gildas advised us to stop the project, referring inquirers to them. For six years we had also produced an annual issue of *Readers' Contributions* which taught us a great deal about their needs, interests, problems, and individual ways of seeking and finding. Much of all this material was used in our first book *Gildas Communicates*[8] followed eight years later by our third, *The Healing Spectrum*[9] containing his teaching on healing and including our individual and group experiences in that field. For by this time not only had we a small working group meeting over many years in different parts of England, but Ruth regularly attended another established group to transmit answers to questions which also fed into the book. Separately and together we gave talks on the work to small groups and larger societies, such as local groups of the Churches' Fellowship for Psychical and Spiritual Studies, the Seekers (Addington Park), the College of Psychic Studies, and the Wrekin Trust, which was then in its earlier stage of development. Ruth still takes workshops

---

8. Ruth White and Mary Swainson, *Gildas Communicates*, first published in 1971 by Spearman, now in 3rd reprint, 1986, The C.W. Daniel Company.

9. Ruth White and Mary Swainson, *The Healing Spectrum*, first published in 1979 (hardback), now in 2nd reprint (paperback), 1986. This book, originally published by Neville Spearman, is now published by The C.W. Daniel Company.

for the Wrekin Trust which is a valuable source of stimulating courses and training in the spiritual nature of humanity.[10] Meanwhile, feeling psychological training and qualification to be an important aspect of her whole work, Ruth obtained a Diploma in Counselling and Guidance at Reading University. She also holds a certificate of study of Transpersonal Perspectives in Counselling.[11] After a couple of years counselling at a natural health clinic, she had a broad basis from which to build the special work she is doing.

I stress this long and thorough preparation because, in my view, it is extremely important that a medium should work from as sound, balanced and healthy a personality as possible. In this way contact may be made with higher levels and frequencies in the subtler worlds without the damage that can too often occur in the case of unprepared and inexperienced psychics.

What Ruth herself understands by mediumship (or 'channelling' as it is termed now, particularly in America) is explained fully in her most recent book.[12]

Both Ruth and I were always healthily critical, even at times sceptical, and perhaps she more than I. I well remember how deeply she would question the validity of her own work. The only comment I could find which always stumped her was, 'Could you, from your present personality, have known or made up teaching of this quality?' 'No.' But we still analysed the origin thoroughly, asking Gildas himself for a discourse on the nature of being, which included the relationship of the incarnate one to the main

---

10. The Wrekin Trust, Runnings Park, Croft Bank, West Malvern, Worcs. WR14 4BP.

11. The Centre for Transpersonal Psychology, 7 Pembridge Place, London W2 4XB.

12. Ruth White, *A Question of Guidance*, The C.W. Daniel Company, 1988.

guide and the higher self.[13] And I wrote the final chapter of that book as a critical evaluation, in as scholarly a fashion as I could, for those who doubted these phenomena.

During this time I learned so much, not only from Gildas, who to some extent took White Eagle's place in helping me personally (they were indeed close in the inner world), but mainly from my relationship with Ruth herself, from her courage, complete dedication, and her love. So thank you Ruth for all that you were and are.

---

13. *Gildas Communicates*, pp. 20–1.

CHAPTER 2

NEW DIMENSIONS IN COUNSELLING AND PSYCHOTHERAPY

Levels in Psychotherapy — The Ego and the Self — The Shadow

As well as from the Readers' Group we had plenty of feedback from papers in *Light*, *The Science of Thought Review* and similar journals, and particularly from our books. Increasingly I came to realise how inadequate for the widespread interest and need was the (then) orthodox level of counselling available. It did not go far enough to meet the deeper psychic and spiritual requirements of so many. Therefore in 1979 I wrote the following article.[14] As the editor suggested in his introduction, 'Psychologies, especially those of a transpersonal nature, will become more and more important in the immediate future in bringing into consciousness the experience of worlds other than the material . . . The linking of different levels of consciousness is an essential aspect of personal growth.'

---

14. First published in *Soluna*, Vol 2. No. 1., 1980. Reproduced in *Light*, Winter 1982.

LEVELS IN PSYCHOTHERAPY

'On which level shall we work?' asked a client returning for more therapy after some years. Here-and-now group interaction was his métier; still to be explored were patterns set up in infancy/childhood, and those deeper levels — reaching beyond the present personality — which caused the re-establishment of such patterns. I explained that, at whatever level we started, by a process similar to induction, any change would affect other levels. There are no rigid boundaries. As I see it, the best principles are first to start where one is, and then to take what comes.

As the New Age approaches, however, the art of psychotherapy seems to be extending from the personal towards the transpersonal; from the limitations of the concept of linear causality to the experience of synchronicity; from materialistic determinism to the realisation of the power of thought and, above all, of creative imagination. Intimations which formerly came only through sleep-dreams are increasingly available to raised consciousness. In this way, some schools practise guided fantasy which is akin to certain methods of led meditation. The linking and transforming power is embodied in the symbol.

For example, by beginning with deliberate visualisation of a form of wholeness, such as the star, rose, or pyramid, integration of the whole psyche is progressively induced. From willed imagery of this kind, the individual may progress to what Jung termed 'active imagination' where the images take on a life of their own so that the conscious ego cannot alter them. (For instance, once I 'saw' what I tried to make into a glorious fountain of light, but it refused to budge from an inkwell with pens sticking out around it!)

There is a natural transition from active imagination to the inner journey where, no matter how the conscious ego may struggle to hasten the pace or to escape, the process follows the rhythm of the inner growth of the whole Self, and in its own time. An interesting feature of this work is that our sense of the time-scale changes. In these inner worlds an immense duration of living may occur in a few minutes of outer clock-time; conversely years of outer life may pass until the subject is ready for changes in the inner.

Co-existent lifetimes

It is a short step from inner journeys to past lives — 'past' in the terminology of our linear time-scale, but possibly co-existent. In my experience, flashes from other lives first emerge like pieces of a jig-saw puzzle, gradually forming a pattern as more incidents fall into place. An increasing amount of research is being done on the many aspects of reincarnation, but in the purely therapeutic context I have found that only those lives — and only those incidents within the lives — which are relevant to the theme to be worked on in the present life are activated.

We find that the process can be trusted. As the themes emerge, together with their essential emotional discharge, the total sequence becomes more meaningful, indicating more obviously the redemptive tasks to be undertaken now. Thus, a physical symptom, inexplicable solely in the context of the present life, may be repeated over and over again in several lifetimes, until we can find the original motive, such as, for example, the inability to forgive oneself, causing the symptom to reappear in life after life as a form of self-punishment.

Work on past lives need not be carried out only in a one-to-one therapeutic setting. Given reasonable maturity and stability, individuals who are committed positively to achieving wholeness, working with one or two friends who feel they have 'met before', can rediscover incidents and traits from past relationships emerging in the far memory of each person, in corroborative fashion, and at the right times for working on them.

Akin to these states of consciousness is what I might term 'parallel living'. Some people, either throughout their whole lives, or only during the period of therapy, may have inner landscapes in which people, animals and events occur, either experienced by the participating subject, or shown as an objective drama on a kind of inner TV screen. These parallel worlds are useful diagnostically as indications of what is going on at present in the outer world; they may also provide helpful guidance to choosing aright. Modifications of one level may affect the other. Or there may be what might be termed a 'remedial zone', set, like inner journeys, in a different time scale from earthly life, where re-growth of the personality can take place, several years of childhood and adolescence being telescoped into one or two years of our time. This is a great help to the therapist since much of the work is done 'over there'. The therapist's job, however, is to make links constantly between the different levels and also between inner and outer, so as to try to prevent too much confusion, and to earth all experience soundly in the here-and-now. Acceptance, integration and application are the keynotes.

Some may be interested in the order in which these varied levels emerge. As yet, my experience is limited, but I would say that classically we work backwards from the here-and-now, through this-life childhood patterns, to guided fantasy, inner journeys and past lives. Parallel worlds, like dreams, may occur at any time, but I have known a case in which past-life flashes came very early on, and were followed by the emotional discharge of buried traumas in the present life together with their application in more conventional therapy. A good deal depends on the nature of the individual and on the initial approach.

Contacting the inner guide

Closely allied to these areas of extended consciousness is the appearance of the inner teacher or guide. Sometimes the figure emerges from guided fantasy when the subject is asked to imagine strongly a helpful being and to listen to what is said. Sometimes the first appearance is in dreams or visions, or on an inner journey. Quite frequently in these times he (or she) can be contacted through what Paul Beard calls 'directed writing'; or words are spoken, dropped singly or in short phrases into the subject's mind, the whole not making sense until the recording is heard afterwards.

Of course, as anyone connected with the training of psychic or extra-sensory faculties knows, the utmost care and discrimination are needed, especially in the early stages when false teachers, or unrecognised aspects of the subject's own personality may be operating. The criterion is always the *quality* of what is given, and the subject comes to know the true teacher by a special vibration. Once established by careful orientation and protection, the messages from the inner teacher can be of inestimable value in the therapeutic context as well as outside it, for the therapist is no longer working alone; the true inner guide knows more surely than either therapist or client what needs to be done, and what is possible at each stage.

It is joyous team work. The therapist can go alongside and learn *with* the client, ceasing to feel too great an ego-responsibility. These inner figures can take over much of the work; especially is this the case on the 'remedial' level once this is contacted and realised as containing experiences as valid as those of outer life.

Not only do these different levels of consciousness interweave each with the other, but also with the outer environment so that, as we progress, an increasing degree of reciprocity is observed between inner perception and outer happenings. Examples of synchronicity, 'the togetherness of things', far exceed the laws of chance. Things happen, we meet people, books are found, all at the significant moment. Gradually the subject becomes aware of him- or herself as contained within a progressively more comprehensive and significant rhythm or matrix, replacing the loss, or lack, of good earthly parents, which may have been traumatic, and giving a great sense of security and meaning to life.

We come to realise that, even if not always consciously, we function on many levels of existence. Further, instead of seeing the commandment to 'Love thy neighbour as thyself' solely as a moral imperative, we discover, as part of the nature of things, that what we are and what we do for ourself we inevitably do for and share with others. Although essentially unique individuals, we are not separate. This becomes actual experience. And then we realise how much there is to be done.

As the changes come on, people are increasingly confused. The limitations of ordinary ego-consciousness make us see change largely in terms of destruction and death. I suggest that one of the 'ways through' may be the living knowledge that we exist also in other worlds.

THE EGO AND THE SELF

When venturing into other worlds of consciousness many pitfalls are found along the way. These can befall all of us explorers so easily that I felt the need to write another paper.

THE CANDLE AND THE SUN[15]

As a psychotherapist researching into further dimensions of awareness, I am particularly concerned with the relationship between ego and greater Self — the candle and the sun. By the ego I understand the little 'I' consciousness, the personality of the present incarnation. The greater being of which the 'I' is but a partial reflection is known in different idioms as 'the deep centre', 'the I AM', 'that of God within us'; but for a group of Jungian psychologists I defined it in this way:

---

15. *Light*, Winter 1980.

The Self, which exists beyond time and space as we know them, includes the distilled essence of many personality aspects of myself and of others, gathered from lives lived in three-dimensional space/time. The limited here-and-now 'I' lives *in reference to this Self*, and the more I can listen to it and integrate with it, using its stored wisdom, the more fully can I function in this world.

Education for relationship between ego and Self

In view of the approaching changes, the mushrooming of groups and schools teaching consciousness expansion is welcome, but, as ever, discrimination is advisable to assess which are sincere and well-founded, which inadequately grounded or even exploiting a need. The 'ego-trip' — or 'ego-trap' — creeps in in subtle ways, until, like watching Aesop's frog, one sometimes wonders *what* is expanding, perhaps by too rapid a forcing which the psyche is as yet not sufficiently balanced to sustain. In my experience, the process of individuation, of becoming a whole person, although certainly it can be aided, takes time if it is to be sound and healthy. Some newcomers expect to be 'changed' in a few months, but this great work takes many years, indeed often a lifetime, which itself may be the final harvesting of the experience of many lives.

It may help to look at a few criteria for assessment in examining the expansion process. These are seen as the ability to resolve pairs of opposites, one pole usually manifesting consciously while the other may well be unconscious and hence more dangerous. Each must find his or her own unique 'middle way', and often the truth of wholeness is an apparent paradox which alone can synthesise these opposites on a higher level of awareness.

(a) *Ego inflation/deflation.* In inflation, the greater is swallowed by the less so as to provide the (usually inadequate) 'I' with a false sense of significance, even of glamour. The compensatory extreme of deflation, falsely imitating humility, can be opting out from being a responsible ego at all — a refusal to commit oneself to the limitations of work within the restriction of one's personality. A mature and strong ego can accept his or her specific earthly service, knowing that they are not alone, not alien, but are lived by a supra-personal being who is one with all things.

(b) *Anxiety/complacency.* In our Western culture the ego has taken on far too great a burden which should be borne by the wiser Self. As we grow and practise contact, it is found, through increasingly meaningful coincidences and otherwise inexplicable happenings, that we are contained in a pattern — a supportive matrix — in which it is possible to relax and hand over, thus reducing stress. The danger is that effort may be abrogated altogether, but such a swing is usually redressed when the flow of the pattern brings us to an area where the ego is challenged to show courage, initiative, even sacrifice.

(c) *Dependence/independence.* These should not normally be compulsive extremes but rather should blend in a growth process. When young in spiritual experience, a formal school training can be helpful; with development we find our own inner directive. The best guru or counsellor cannot know, as can the inner guide, what is the specific path and timing suitable for each individual student, and reputable schools will help the student to make critical but increasingly reliable contact with his or her own source. There is, however, a seductive inertia which leads some of us to avoid the individual way and to remain a dependent child; if an irresponsible guru 'cashes in' on this weakness — beware!

Other criteria will spring to mind. It may also help if seekers ask themselves the simple question, 'What am I

41

doing this *for*? This power, knowledge, insight, that I am developing, how shall I use it?' If to serve God and humanity, then all is well, but it can be employed on the left-hand path, which may even masquerade as service to God and humanity. I have found that too much 'do-goodery' for the wrong reasons may be worse than open 'do-badery'.

Another useful question is, 'What difficulties am I experiencing in surrender? Why cannot I trust life, trust the pattern, and let go?' Psychological help may be needed here, for the weak or unformed ego, still vulnerable, may defend itself by moat and drawbridge, or even by anticipatory attack. The underlying fear is usually that it will be shamed or rejected, invaded or possessed. Or do we perhaps, like Tinker Bell, feel that we exist only in the opinions, values and beliefs of other people? And that if we hand over to the Self we may cease to be there at all? Like the revolving, differently-coloured glass of a lighthouse, some feel that ships (people) recognise them only by the correct colours they show, forgetting the stability of the central white light within. But this again is a matter of growth, of progressive detachment from the many-coloured personality as we learn to love and value ourselves to the degree that we love and value others, no more and no less. How do we see our own ego in the total picture?

Readers of Gildas' teachings, striving to live more and more from the inexhaustible resources of health and energy of the deep centre, once asked him about the place of the ego in the New Age. Should the ego be encouraged to develop, especially in youth when degree of ego strength is held to be one of the main criteria of mental health? Or can one, in the New Age, function without it, living entirely from the 'Monad' as one reader suggested, by-passing the separate ego altogether? Should the ego be seen as 'the enemy' to be fought and crushed throughout life, as another reader believed? Or should it be developed and then formed into a strong but flexible channel for the higher Self to use,

42

working together in harmony? Gildas gave his point of view:[16]

> The ego will continue to be necessary as long as the karmic law is in operation, and the New Age, which we presently expect, does not bring the ending of karma. It brings a new understanding, the entrance into a new breadth of vision, the acceptance of different values, a shift of consciousness, and a new ease of communication. The need to incarnate on to the physical plane, however, will continue and the karmic law will continue. The ego — the personality — is the vehicle through which the karmic law operates; without this the lessons of life and experience would not be learned.
>
> As experience and learning grow, so the ego loses its importance to the individual and he passes into a new region of consciousness, a new phase of incarnation; but the ego is a very important part of the totality and should not be despised for its limitations, but rather wondered at for that which in its fullest strength it can accomplish.
>
> The ideal and most comfortable situation whilst experiencing earth incarnation is for the individual to reach that stage where the ego, strongly rooted in the light, can open up sufficiently to let through frequent glimpses of and contact with the greater, higher Self. Complete loss or superseding of the ego comes to few, and it is not altogether a comfortable achievement whilst still on earth. The New Age to come will bring about a new ease of achieving the ideal relationship between the ego and the infinite, but the ego will continue to be very necessary to the complete, integrated, earth-incarnate individual.

THE SHADOW

In order to relate fully to the Self, the personal ego needs to become, in itself, as whole and fully conscious as possible, otherwise blocks will occur. This entails preliminary work on what Jung calls the 'Shadow', that part of our personality which we would rather not see. Ignored or repressed, it can be dangerous, but if recognised and accepted it can be

---

16. Ruth White and Mary Swainson, *The Healing Spectrum*, pp. 183–4.

transformed so that we become integrated, rounded, human beings. Again, perhaps I can best contribute from my own experience, called forth by a request from the editor of *Soluna* for personal views of this phenomenon:[17]

* * * *

You ask how I, a Jungian psychotherapist, view the Shadow.

Many years ago, Dr Graham Howe asked me to speak at his Open Way centre in London on 'Who is The Enemy?' (This is an exercise I can recommend!) From the 'dark' part of my psyche, and as spontaneously as possible, I drew on the blackboard a huge, lethargic saurian whose small head displayed drooping, seductive eyelashes and a placating, inoffensive smile to prove how harmless it was. Its tail, however, curved over its back with a sting like that of a scorpion, symbolising the brooding vindictiveness of this over-sensitive creature who became ill and inert if faced with moral blame.

Characteristically, my pioneering, Arien, conscious ego, brought up on Kipling's *If*, compensated by compulsive over-drive to the point of extreme exhaustion, propitiating tyrannical god-figures by duty and do-goodery. Understandably both of us, ego and Shadow, found it difficult to find who we really were, which was which; to become a whole person; to trust life.

In working on this fascinating creature, fascinating because its imprisoned energy exerted so strong a pull that I *needed* it in order to survive, I learned first to feel compassion, to see it not as The Enemy but as The Friend. My analyst, quoting Prospero, stressed recognition and acceptance: 'This thing of darkness I acknowledge mine.' Then came valuing; I had not realised how immensely strong this saurian could be, were it not paralysed by fear, and if it could be transmuted. My analyst explained that these primitive creatures *want* to evolve into higher forms even if change implies death and rebirth. So my task has been to let go of both the crippling anxiety (with its underlying resentment) and the frenetic over-compensation, thus releasing and training the freed energy. The only way, I found, has been to hand over the whole ego/Shadow complex to the greater Self who makes use of *all* aspects of the personality for purposes beyond ourselves, ignoring our 'moral' division into opposites. At

---

17. *Soluna*, Vol. 3, No. 6, 1982.

seventy-four I am *still* struggling to hand over, slowly learning to trust the unifying process.

That is the first stage. When the personality is reasonably whole and free, we are strong enough to face the collective, even the cosmic Shadow. It is wise, however, to take on only that share of it which we can handle or else, in over-enthusiasm for world redemption, we may be lost. Here is the present meaning of the adventures of the knights of old, penetrating dark forests in search of the Grail, the way of inner exploration. The Shadow is described as 'dark' because unknown, not because it is necessarily evil. Indeed Jung has indicated that in the Shadow lies the gold, 'the treasure hard to attain', 'the pearl of great price'. It is that part of the *prima materia* of life needing to be made conscious. Often it terrifies because it extends beyond our present limited understanding or control; by our definition it appears chaotic, a *massa confusa*, usually requiring an altered state of consciousness and a new kind of order to provide meaning and form. Yet, given sufficient courage and persistence, we can channel its energy to bring through invaluable insights not only for ourselves but for the planet. Indeed, for some 'old souls' who are redeeming their share of the collective Shadow through deep meditation, inner journeys, or work on lives far distant in our time, the experience can be not of the unknown but of recognising values and qualities of life, long forgotten; their chief difficulty lies in communicating and mediating the truths perceived to our present restricted attitudes. Our task is to become open to meet them. This, as I see it, is the 'great work' of our time. And then, to quote Ruth White in a recent lecture, we shall discover not the dark, but 'the bright, the creative Shadow, that which brings newness into us and understanding'.

Whether working on personal, collective, or cosmic levels (all of which we find mirror one another), there comes a moment when, in a flash, transcending the dichotomy of Consciousness/Shadow, we glimpse that stillness of pure being where the interplay of apparent opposites is no longer necessary for the growth and education of incarnate humanity. In this greater light which being inclusive casts no shadow, we see quite simply and without judgement that what is *is*, and is for a purpose. Only then can we learn to trust the whole pattern of existence, dark and light, life and death.

CHAPTER 3

EXPLORING INNER WORLDS

An Historical Perspective — A Practical, Present-day Approach to other Worlds — The Need for Education of the Psychic Faculties — Preparation for Mediumship

AN HISTORICAL PERSPECTIVE

'Why', some more extraverted people have asked, 'should all this psychological work be necessary? It can be painful, slow, and take much time and energy. It can even lead to unhealthy self-centredness instead of flowing out in good works. If only outer conditions were improved then there would be no need for such labour.'

Up to a point of course this is true; sick, starving and homeless people need practical help first. But 'if only' can be wishful thinking. Looking back in history we can see that social, political and economic plans, utopias, blue-prints of ideal communities — any structure in fact that is imposed from without — will tend eventually to collapse unless the participants are ready for it in their inner beings. To be viable, in my opinion, the outer form needs to grow organically from what its members *are*, even if (as is usual and to be accepted as a learning process) there are many growing pains, losses and changes. It is the inner-directed, inspired thinkers, scientists, and artists of all kinds who have provided those quantum leaps for humanity in every aspect of living, from philosophical and religious insights to the material discoveries which facilitate practical living.

Again, some have questioned, 'Why stress these relatively new-fangled psychological methods as if they were the only way?' Of course they are not the only way; as a wise man once told me, 'Life analyses you.' But they happen to be *one* way which, as a Jungian psychotherapist, it has been my task to offer. Further, it is clear to any student of anthropology investigating the traditional wisdom of former cultures that special training of certain gifted individuals to experience other states of consciousness, and then to transmit the knowledge to those of the group able to take it, has always been prevalent. In particular were the schools of the ancient mysteries, involving long and arduous temple training with its progressive initiations. These go back to Greek, Egyptian, and further (we have some reason to believe) to Atlantean times, among other civilisations now lost to us. In them, priests and priestesses, seers and oracles were an intrinsic and essential part of the culture.[18] It is conceivable that present day psychological methods, especially at the transpersonal level, are just one new idiom for similar training. I have found corroborative parallels in several cases, notably with Louisa's sister Jessica, but that is another story.

Two specific aspects described here certainly have historical precedents:

(a) *Inner Journeys.* Even in relatively recent times, and in Europe, we find three well known figures ranging from the early fourteenth to the eighteenth centuries. Dante, typically at the critical mid-life period, journeyed through Hell, Purgatory, and Paradise. Bunyan, during a long, introverted period in prison, wrote

---

18. See Jon Klimo, *Channeling*, Thorsons (Aquarian Press), 1988, Chapter 2, for a useful summary.

Pilgrim's Progress. And Swedenborg's inner experiences, recorded in *Heaven and Hell*, resulted in a range of innovative works on many aspects of life.[19] Although their form of expression and symbolism varied, reflecting the ethos and climate of thought of their times, these three have much in common at a basic archetypal level, both with one another and with those at the present day who dare to go upon such a journey.

The value of inner journeys to society is that they bring a further dimension of insight into our three-dimensional space/time world. The pattern of withdrawal and return does not make for healing and wholeness until these insights are fully earthed in the here-and-now. But I have written a full analysis of the process in the first chapter of *Seven Inner Journeys*.

(b) **The guide, inner teacher or helper. Inspiration from higher sources.** Traditionally, one does not journey alone. Dante was first led by Virgil, then by Beatrice. Bunyan had the companionship of Faithful, then Hopeful. Swedenborg was illumined by higher beings and spirits. In more recent times, Jung, during his journey within, related closely to his own inner teacher whom he called Philemon, and with whom he held long conversations.[20] To go further back, the Greeks recognised their Daimon (not to be confused with 'demon'). Few artists or writers, even at the present day, would deny the creative value of what the Greeks called their Muse.

At a less personal, more cosmic level, the great

---

19. See Wilson Van Dusen, *The Presence of Other Worlds*, Swedenborg Foundation, 1974. This book was recommended by the well-known psychologist Carl Rogers as appealing 'especially to those persons who are not afraid of the inner psychic world.'

20. C.G. Jung, *Memories, Dreams, Reflections*, Fontana (Flamingo), 1983, pp. 207–10.

religions have all recognised spiritual inspiration from the ultimate source of being, in whatever way it was perceived and received, or transmitted through intermediaries. Thus the Hindus saw Brahman as the universal, unmanifest, transcendent principle, to be made known through Atman, the immanent divine spark in the world and in humankind, and so on to the many gods and goddesses representing various and sometimes dualistic powers and attributes. The Hebrew prophets heard 'the word of the Lord'. Jesus spoke and healed directly from 'The Father in me'. Mohammed acted as prophet of Allah, transmitting the Koran. These and many, many others showed the way by means of the highest possible extension of their consciousness to reach the nature of the creative infinite, whatever name it be given: God; the Great White Spirit; the I AM; the Word, the Light, the Life; or (to quote Dante), 'Love, that moves the sun and every star.' This 'exploration into God' implied increasing perception of the purpose of incarnate life; also of the pattern operating in all creation, such as is felt in the flow of the Tao; and again the means of finding those truths as, for instance, by following the eightfold path of the Buddha.

Further, as well as merely following set teachings given by the great prophets and seers, recognition has always been given to the immense degree of their personal preparation for such insights. Therefore, most religions have their branches schooling aspirants who desire to perceive these truths themselves by hard individual training and growth. Examples are the Zen Buddhists, the Sufis, and the Christian mystics who search for, and learn to communicate with, what may be termed 'The Christ Within'. Some experience this illumination directly, others through a spiritual hierarchy of messengers who may be regarded as saints, guides, or helpers from many levels. One of the most rapidly growing schools in the West, linking spirit with body, is that of Hindu yoga, adapted to our specific needs. Of special interest for this book is the recommendation of Indian yogis to guard against the 'siddhis' which they see as the lower psychic aspects that can be activated on the earlier stages of the path.

It is clear then that, in practice, relationship to the inner source may come directly, or more likely through many levels, according to the degree of purity and development of the receiver, like attracting like. Thus, experience of other worlds can range from the nearest approach we can make to the sublime realisation of the oneness of all things, to that appalling state of diversity, polarised conflict, multiplicity, and even possession where indeed the Daimon can become a Demon. Truly, 'In my Father's house are many mansions.'

A PRACTICAL PRESENT-DAY APPROACH TO OTHER WORLDS

If we work today, in a largely materialistic society, with potentially spiritually gifted individuals, immense care is necessary. Especially is this so in view of the current explosion in the psychic field (siddhis). Not only the yogis, but many of the more orthodox Christian churches do not condone mediumship, regarding it — understandably enough if judged only by inferior quality or by its abuse — as 'of the Devil'. This attitude could be confusing for many potential mediums who are also practising Christians. In letters from readers of our books, Ruth and I received many queries from, for instance, one partner of an otherwise good marriage. Usually she (but sometimes he) suffered acutely because of having to choose between being true to the psychic aspect of herself, or feeling that she should go along with her partner's beliefs. The issue was even more acute when these beliefs were also her own, hence creating an inner conflict as well. Especially was this the case with clergymen's wives who felt loyalty to their husbands' profession as an added factor. And some clergy and ministers found the conflict existing within themselves, complicated also by the fear that their careers might be affected (see Appendix).

The problem is not confined to religious differences. Some families have split up because the more rigidly materialistic members accuse the 'sensitive' member of being dotty, or at worst actually insane. This attitude can be particularly prevalent among those in the medical world who hold that the brain creates the mind, instead of the mind using the physical brain as an instrument, or better still in mutual cooperation, as parts of a whole.

In replying, although each case varied, I used to advise the sensitive first to accept and respect the different attitude of the partner, which was perhaps fitting for his present incarnation. In some cases, possibly, he was at present *incapable* of understanding senses beyond the conventional five. Try to understand the deeper reasons for his attitude. For herself, it was often wise to keep quiet while yet remaining true to her own inner vision, rather than increasing the opposition by provoking an overt holy war. However, if it were felt that action should be taken, there was no harm in leaving a carefully chosen, well-reasoned bridge-book lying around. The partner's free will would then be respected, but if he did feel inwardly drawn to pick it up (which often happened) this might lead to a creative discussion.

It is most important to avoid self-betrayal, or else the sensitive might become ill. If possible it would increase confidence if she were to make contact with others in similar positions; it was here that our annual issue of *Readers' Contributions*, while it lasted, provided a rich forum for sharing. Further, in the case of religious scruples, some were able to join local branches of the Churches' Fellowship for Psychical and Spiritual Studies.[21] In this way, often to their surprise, they found that even within their own church an increasing number of clergy were now accepting the *positive* use of higher psychic faculties to aid spiritual growth, for example in meditation groups, healing services, and even exorcism.

A frequent question is, 'Are the guides real or imaginary?' And one of the main criticisms levelled at potential mediums is that they are losing touch with reality. I fully accept that this can be a problem, especially where, in false motivation such as the need to escape or impress, the individual does succumb to glamour. This tends, in my experience, to occur more often when the sensitive feels completely isolated, encountering only those with an ordinary three-dimensional view of reality and who therefore deny his or her own incipient perceptions.

To a certain extent this problem is a semantic one. Personally, I would challenge the accusers first to define their terms: 'What do you mean by "reality"?' Eventually, they may be prepared to admit that beyond the narrow span of human five-sense perception, through which their reality is defined, lie further areas. Research on animals indicates that many not only possess wider and keener powers than do humans within our sensory wave-band, but also they can sense and use more subtle signals such as the earth's magnetic currents. This research is extending into even more subtle fields. How much more then should the *Homo sapiens*, now facing the test of coming of age as a full human being,[22] involving progressive understanding of a spiritual nature, be aware of the need to develop and use the higher sense levels? Perception of a further order of reality does not deny

---

21. Headquarters: The Priory, 44 High Street, New Romney, Kent TN28 8BZ.

22. See Gildas' Conclusion in Ruth White, *A Question of Guidance*. Also Chapter 4 for fuller treatment of this topic with practical suggestions.

'down here' reality; it simply increases the range.[23]

Where discarnate guides and helpers are concerned, their relatively less dense subtle bodies (see Glossary) need human senses developed to a wide range of equivalent levels in order to 'see' and 'hear' them. Further, not only our senses but our conceptual models also need modification and extension. For example, one questioner, commenting on the assumption of one person, one guide, calculated an astronomical number of separate guides required, when he did his sums by using our normal three-dimensional arithmetic. But, as in the image of Plato's cave (or a cinema), our reality may well be a projection onto a limited-dimensional screen of a multi-dimensional reality, where head-counts do not apply numerically in this way.[24] So we need to stretch our present conceptual framework to imagine creatively a more comprehensive state of being.

With many of these problems in mind, a team of nine of us, including five incarnates and four discarnates, wrote a symposium on 'Inner Guidance'.[25] This included a most interesting analysis from Gildas of the technical difficulties encountered in communication from a guide's point of view.[26] The following introduction, entitled 'Communication with the Inner Guide' was my own contribution.

* * * *

As the new energies infiltrate our planet, causing expanded awareness, not only 'special' sensitives but more and more so-called ordinary people find themselves living

---

23. See Louisa's view (p. 132) and Nabraham's Conclusion (p. 141).

24. See pp. 95–7 where Nabraham replies to a similar question concerning over-population.

25. *Soluna*, Vol. 3, No. 3, 1981.

26. Taken from *Gildas Communicates*, pp. 216–8.

and relating inwardly in strange new ways. Hopefully, these experiences reflect the higher worlds, although the present explosion of mental illness witnesses also to the reverse side of the coin. Psychic phenomena proliferate, yet orthodox education fails either to understand the psychic faculty or to develop it spiritually. Of course there are schools teaching esoteric disciplines, but in too many there is the danger of the pupil becoming over-dependent on the external guru.

I suggest that the psychic uprush itself may well indicate its own specific need: that of inner training by the pupil's individual source. In going inwards, some people prefer the channel of an accepted religion or cult; other strong souls venture to confront the archetypes or even the Source directly; but from my experience I cannot over-estimate the value — whether in psychotherapy or any other discipline — of first recognising and then working closely with the inner, personal guide, the wayshower on the path. In a technique not primarily psychological, Steinbrecher[27] warns the seeker not to contact the high energies of the archetypes without due mediation by the guide, who knows his or her pupil's strengths and weaknesses at each stage; otherwise there is the danger of being unconsciously overwhelmed by the archetype, as for instance in the animus-ridden woman, the anima-possessed man, or an ego inflated by the Sun-Self, instead of relating harmoniously to it. If the pace is forced, there may be severe physical or mental repercussions and often understandable rebellion from the unready ego. Only the inner guide can assess the slow, careful development needed, often prescribing pauses for rest and stabilising.

The inner guide may emerge in dreams, visions, painting, meditation, guided or spontaneous imagery, automatic or

---

27. Edwin C. Steinbrecher, *The Inner Guide Meditation*, Thorsons (The Aquarian Press), 1988.

directed writing and speaking. The main criterion in assessing validity is the quality of the communication, but there are many pitfalls. Beginners may become obsessed by their 'voices', at worst indulging at all hours, unprotected, in compulsive automatism, the messages insisting on bizarre behaviour and actions. When the guide lays claim to a great name, even 'screaming' at his or her pupil when warning of dire consequences if the dicta are not obeyed, then is the time to seek reliable outer advice, and above all to work on the personality in order to achieve as much growth, balance and integrity as possible, so as to be in a position to discriminate. The true guides do not impersonate the great. Their vibrations which, with practice, can always be sensed, are those of gentle, unconditional love and wisdom, always combined with respect for free will. Even after considerable schooling, parts of an otherwise objective and true message may be distorted; this usually occurs when the pupil's personal emotions, desires and fears are involved.

In training, the pupil needs to orient (tune in) to the highest frequency of vibration manageable, calling confidently for protection from false communicators, visualising the true light and the true guide. Pupils should then become as open and passive as possible during the period of reception, stilling the mind and emotions. Critical reviewing is a different process, having its place afterwards. Later, in applying the teaching received, it is crucial to retain balance between inner vision and outer action, earthing soundly every higher perception, at the right time. The process of earthing is the result of a long, close, and hard-working relationship. As one of our discarnate contributors, Epidron, said to his incarnate co-worker, Janet, 'I feel that ours is a partnership. I could not convey such truths to you (thence you to others) without the loving and careful preparation you have undertaken at some cost to yourself. You, the instrument, are being prepared to live out your inner experience in the world, and it is right that we should be allied in readers' minds from the beginning.'

In my experience I find that communication with the guide varies according to three factors:

(a) **The stage reached.** Usually personal advice comes first, directed to the pupil's growth needs; more general teaching comes later.

(b) **The nature of the pupil.** The guides are both favoured and limited by the equipment of their human partners. Thus the teaching may be expressed philosophically or through poetic imagery; in scientific concepts; in parables from daily life; or in many other modes.

(c) **The level of progress** of the teaching guide or archetypal figure encountered.

THE NEED FOR EDUCATION OF THE PSYCHIC FACULTIES

The question of levels is all-important. In Indian culture, which in many ways is so much older and wiser spiritually than our own, it may well be possible to by-pass psychism. But in the West, ignorance and suppression (as in witch hunts not so long ago) have often led to its emergence in inferior ways. At its worst are the horrific rituals of black magic — sometimes associated with unmentionable details of child abuse — that are still only too active at the present time.

People are very confused. Early in 1986 a reader of the journal *New Humanity* wrote asking what was the difference between the terms 'psychic' and 'spiritual'. Since the editor requested other readers to 'have a go', I wrote the following letter as a basis for discussion. I did not attempt to define spirituality except in terms of developing wholeness of being and of the true love/wisdom which is a result of raising human energies to the higher centres. But I did attempt to show that psychic faculties are not in themselves necessarily wrong or low grade. As with all forms of energy, everything depends on the way we use them:[28]

> I would regard psychic functions such as clairvoyance, clairaudience, awareness of other existences, etc., as innate gifts varying in kind and degree among individuals in the same way as intelligence, artistic, mathematical or other specific abilities. It seems probable that all 'gifts' have been developed in former lives by hard work and careful training. They are incarnated into the present life through psychological heredity via suitable parents, and then (ideally) accepted and fostered — but not over-emphasised as odd — by the environmental ethos of the community, as in many American Indian, Celtic and other groups. Unfortunately, in our materialistic Western society in general, the psychic faculty has been denied (particularly in small children: 'It's only your imagination'), derided and repressed, with the inevitable result that it manifests in the cruder forms of fortune-telling or becomes drastically abused as in black magic. I agree completely with Dr Guirdham that unrecognised and repressed psychic energy lies at the root of much of our present psychological imbalance. However, the current universal interest in psychic phenomena reinforces the need for recognition and redemption of this energy which in itself is morally neutral and therefore available for evil or good, for illness or for more extensive health enriching human potential.
>
> And this is where spiritual aims are essential, although first must come conscious responsibility, direction and education, for, insofar as these psychic faculties remain split off, they tend to manifest in spontaneous and uncontrollable ways. An example is the excess of 'free floating' psychic energy, especially in young people, available for poltergeist phenomena (uncanny sounds, sights, or movement of objects). Or voices insist on too frequent so-called automatic writing, often in the false name of some high authority and urging bizarre behaviour. It is the *compulsive* quality which is so alarming to the subject who feels that nothing can be done to stop an apparent invasion beyond his control. Some perceive themselves as involuntarily open to low grade — or at best harmless but unhelpful — spirits whose desire to communicate causes unceasing and unendurable babble. A friend passing through this stage with some

---

28. *New Humanity*, No. 70, 1986.

detachment and humour called it 'Paddington Station'.

The immediate need is for protection, healing, understanding, control, and diversion of the energies into positive channels such as disciplined study or a creative activity like painting, writing or joining a reliable training group. In this way the faculty may eventually be used for healing, teaching, or even directly as high grade mediumship to help others. Gentle, balanced, breathing exercises, visualisation to raise and balance the energies, regular meditation: all these are helpful but should be done at first only under careful guidance.

To quote an instance, one client who sometimes found herself floating out of her body was pursued by flashing lights, sounds of footsteps and beings sitting on the bed when the whole room became electric with power. First-aid methods concentrated on protection: sealing of the centres (especially the solar plexus), the whole aura and the room, complemented by prayer and invocation of the true light. The energy was then directed into psychotherapy aimed at integrating and strengthening the vehicle of her personality. This phase lasted for many years, involving inner journeys and recall of former lives in some of which she had experienced intensive training of spiritual and psychic qualities, for in those times evolved and trained psychic powers were part of spiritual disciplines. During the course of this work she found her main inner teacher and other long-term companions of the spirit who helped her regain her former knowledge and to reach, in the present life, a level which was *not* an escape to Cloud 9 but involved much painful earthing of all that she recaptured, each memory rigorously tested at every stage in outer tasks and human relationships. As a nurse, counsellor, and qualified yoga teacher, she had ample opportunity to put her recovered gifts into practice.

What is needed then, in our society, is acceptance, comprehension, and above all education of the psychic faculty. There are now many books, teachers, good yoga classes, groups, conference centres, all catering for this need, though the individual will choose critically according to taste and level. Particularly recommended is Paul Beard's paper on methods of handling 'Directed Writing' published in *New Humanity* October/November 1979.[29] Some Eastern teachers advise by-passing the 'siddhis' (psychic powers) in order not to be diverted from attainment of spiritual levels; in a culture that has catered for spiritual education over centuries, such an attitude is

---

29. Photocopies available at £1.00 from *New Humanity*, 51A York Mansions, Prince of Wales Drive, London SW11 4BP.

understandable. In the West we draw from Christianity which *originally* saw powers such as healing, miracles, casting out devils (exorcism), inspiration, and similar positive abilities, as an integral part of spirituality; only later were they split off in witch hunts and so 'went bad'. Naturally, these neglected functions now erupt negatively or cannot be ignored or by-passed. They need to be valued, trained and transformed, so that, as an essential aspect of the total psyche, they can heal the self, others, and the earth itself.

PREPARATION FOR MEDIUMSHIP

One — and one only — use of the trained and educated psychic function is mediumship. Others are healing (of humans, animals, plants, and the earth); divination; release of earthbound discarnates; exorcism of possessing entities; and many other specialised forms of service.

The term 'medium' needs clarification. In a recent book[30] Jon Klimo, writing in America, attributes the word largely to British use, restricting it to describe those sensitives who bring through deceased human beings. He prefers the (to him) broader term 'channel' which 'covers communication with all other kinds of intelligences not associated with embodied minds or with physical reality.'

This distinction, I would suggest, is largely a matter of terminology. Many British sensitives or 'mediums' are certainly not restricted to giving evidence of survival, although that can be a very important part of their work especially in bereavement. In the UK valuable information and new, illuminating ideas have been brought through from higher sources. Even from my own limited but direct experience I have mentioned White Eagle (through Grace Cooke), Gildas (through Ruth White) and there are many, many more. In this present book Nabraham has indicated that he belongs

---

30. Jon Klimo, *Channeling*, Thorsons (The Aquarian Press), 1988, especially p. 304.

to a teaching brotherhood although he explains that some discarnate groups specialise in different branches of the work (see pp. 81–2). My own feeling is that the terms applied to those who mediate between levels are less important than the quality of wisdom imparted. Surely, in appraising psychic communications, value and meaning are the essential criteria?

But what of the origin? What is meant by 'higher sources'? Klimo creates a specific term 'open channelling' to define 'the ability to act as a vehicle for thought, images, feeling and information coming from a source that is beyond the individual's self and from beyond ordinary reality (as we know them).' He believes the two most universal forms of open channelling to be intuition and creativity, recognising that 'the human mind has unlimited resources on which to draw.' Further, he suggests that the extension of the individual mind into the universal mind is something we can all aim to develop. Is it therefore conceivable that sensitives are those who point the rest of us at least along *one* way towards this goal?

Modern physicists[31] increasingly admit that the mind of the experimenter, observer, (or medium?) is a vital factor in the findings of the experiment. The further our awareness reaches, the closer become so-called objective and subjective modes of perception. Intuition is indeed a crucial function; the sensitive often *recognises* what comes through as something which, at a superconscious level, has always been known, yet without knowing at the personality level *that* she or he knows. It would seem that in these increasingly subtle, even ideoplastic realms, we cannot apply ordinary three-dimensional standards of assessment. To take an example, from our down-here world, where we are caught in the learning process of tension between apparent op-

---

31. See for instance Fritjof Capra, *The Turning Point*, Fontana (Flamingo), 1985. Also Arthur J. Ellison (see p. 146).

posites, we tend to ask too many questions of the either/or variety, whereas at a more holistic, comprehensive level the answer is often 'both'.

In the Evaluation at the end of this book (see p. 127), the three of us, Louisa, Jessica and myself cogitate on this difficult fringe of knowledge. For example, the separation of 'self' and 'other' — so obvious when each is bounded by skin — is one of those potentially divisive concepts needing a deeper vision of truth when we struggle to comprehend the nature of group souls. And beyond them lies the still greater degree of unity of being where the source of wisdom is available to those who can reach it.

So, in the preparation of student sensitives (channels or mediums), I have found a progressive interaction between the psychological state and the quality of what is mediated. In the early stage, or in the case of an unbalanced sensitive, personal needs may influence the messages; these are particularly dangerous when they are still unconscious and projected so that slanted directives and trite answers to questions are attributed to 'guidance'. At the other end of the scale, a developed, integrated and experienced medium can mediate that quality of life and beauty which sheds the light of true (not escapist) reality into our relatively dark and suffering world. To live *from* that light while yet *in* the incarnate condition is surely the task of those who are sufficiently sensitive to link the two states of being.

A wise man, who has had extensive experience with sensitives, rightly told me that no non-medium can teach mediums because we cannot know what is going on behind the scenes. However, he felt that a developed medium can still improve the quality of transmission by removing any personal blocks, and that is where we can help. I fully agree.

Ample provision for the training of sensitives by professional mediums is given at the College of Psychic Studies in London. But what of those living at a distance, unable to attend formal development classes? And what of the increasing numbers who do not know where to turn in order

61

to handle their rapidly emerging, often frightening, psychic abilities, yet who long to make contact with higher truths and to serve?

Not being psychic (although intuitive) myself, I realise that I lack the qualifications of those teachers at the College. All I can say is that in the case of the few who have come my way I have done my best. And in the present work I give my heartfelt thanks to Nabraham and his group on the other side who have done most of the training.

Part Two of this book is a record of the early work of Louisa, and later also of her sister Jessica, in practising communication on subjects of general interest. Both sisters have undergone plenty of rich, intense, and often painful experiences in jobs, poverty, raising families, and learning about relationships. So now, in their forties, they feel ready for wider service. We all agree that as full an experience of outer life as possible should precede and continue alongside the work of mediumship in understanding and serving others.

The record is offered partly for general interest to stimulate open-minded discussion of the methods used and the subjects covered in the exercises. More specifically, it is intended as a contribution for research purposes to those studying the early preparation of sensitives. The growing quality of the communications — the problems as the questions asked become more subtle and penetrating — all this may form some criteria for readers' consideration and judgement.

PART TWO

A LIFE ON THE PATH

CHAPTER 4

LOUISA'S STORY

From the Beginning — Preparation and Training — Further Tests and Achievements — An Experiment

FROM THE BEGINNING

by Louisa

As a small child I remember being aware of and sensitive to discrepancies between what people said and what they were actually feeling. These early insights revealed to me the conflicting and labyrinthine nature of relationships both between and within everyone around me. I lived in my imagination and was completely happy to play with invisible friends, fairies and animals. Perhaps an early solitude of nature allowed me the expressive freedom to communicate with my innermost feelings and fantasies. Later as an adolescent I prayed fervently and intensely whenever I was moved by the pain and sufferings I saw clearly in everyday faces and scenes. Whether it was a robin who had lost his mate or the earthquakes and hunger of the Developing World, I sang it all to the heavens and the powers that move the universe. I had no formal belief in a God, but a continual desire to implore and commune with that which was beyond my sight.

At twenty-eight I became interested in psychic phenomena, occult and mystic teachings, became a disciple to a fashionable guru, and read endlessly anything I could find which might offer me 'a way'. I was not lost or desperate but I was inquisitive and hungry. I was a member of a psychic rescue circle and through another medium was shown how to operate a planchette. I played with this for some months before I found I could write more easily by simply holding the pen and allowing the words to form.

The development of mediumship was gradual. As I took more seriously the moral relationship between myself and those I lived and worked with, so did the quality and depth of the writing increase. My reading was extensive in the field of psychology, especially C.G. Jung and R.D. Laing; later Ruth White's and Mary Swainson's books, especially *Seven Inner Journeys*, gave me a path to follow. Prior to the writing, I worked for almost three years on Jungian active imagination. These inner journeys contributed greatly to my understanding of myself and also developed a sense of mission or service to humankind. Through this work and my enduring relationship with my sister Jessica, and Mary, I have grown in inner strength and yet remain open to the inevitable suffering which accompanies expanded sensitivity. It has been a rewarding journey, and I would only say to anyone who begins this path, 'There is a beauty in life; we perceive it rarely enough. That beauty expands as the path is followed, but yet there is also pain, the depths of which we must plumb. It is not a path for those who wish for ease, yet even so tranquillity, peace and joy will come to you at unexpected moments.'

PREPARATION AND TRAINING

by Mary

It has been said by a very experienced and wise man that 'The two most important qualities needed for true mediumship are dedication and character discipline, both far more important than the natural gift so often wasted by the lack of these.' He also appreciated the part that psychotherapy can play: 'Incipient mediums could hardly have a better training for self-discipline.'

As she describes, Louisa has been naturally sensitive all her life, so she has the gift. Discipline she has experienced in plenty. I first met her in 1976 in connection with her elder sister Jessica who was then starting to work intensively and in depth with me; this has continued, though to a steadily decreasing extent, in recent years. Throughout the earlier stages, until Jessica gained confidence in her own direct contact and channelling, Louisa helped us both by her mediumship and mutually shared insights. So despite being at one remove, Jessica's inner work was an invaluable experience for Louisa.

From 1978, at thirty-one, Louisa and I started a few informal talks in depth on her own inner and outer life, forming a growing friendship. By that time her inner journey had already been going on, and I found how much she had already achieved on her own in order to clear, balance and educate her personality as a sound instrument for whatever form of service she would finally undertake. She continued alone until 1982 when she underwent a year's course of weekly psychotherapy with me. This was intensive and radical; later it decreased to less frequent, follow-up sessions. An important factor is that this development was never forced; natural phases of growth and experience have always been respected and used. Another factor in balancing her personality, which is naturally strongest in the feeling function, was to commit herself in 1982 to the mental discipline of taking, at a college of further education in only one year, two A levels and one (essential) O level, gaining an 'A' grade in all three. This was immediately followed by a three-year course, as a 'mature student', for a degree in psychology at a university.

Throughout the time I have known her, Louisa has worked with one or other of her inner teachers. In the initial stages and helping with the journey was Septimus who did not explain who he was until much later, well after Nabraham had become the main communicator. But in early December 1983 apparently Nabraham was 'in retreat', preparing with his colleagues for the Christmas festival. Sensing a change of vibration, Louisa questioned who was writing. Septimus identified himself as her former helper and explained:

'We are the circle of protectors who watch over the teachers and guides in their meditations before the great time of blessing. We sit around them and keep the peace between such as yourself, and even ward away those darker souls who would interfere with their meditations. We are intermediaries between the two worlds. As such, we are learners or pupils to the guides.'[1] This is particularly relevant in view of what Nabraham says on the function of intermediaries (see page 90), and interesting that in her development Louisa should contact first the pupil, then the teaching guide.

Nabraham (pronounced Narbraham) first emerged as Jessica's inner way-shower and teacher. He claimed (and this was experienced in detail in one of Jessica's main recalls) to have been the father of them both in a past life. So here we have a (perhaps unique?) example of a shared guide and communicator, leading to some interesting experiments.

When more abstract, deeper information is required, the messages come from the whole group of Nabraham's teaching colleagues who often prepare carefully beforehand, and then the pronoun 'we' is invariably used:

'We are the light bearers of whom Nabraham is one. We speak with a group voice.'

The method of communication is that of writing, in the early years coming in a completely different script from Louisa's own, letters and words joined continuously, sen-

---

1. See *Light*, Spring 1985, note on the Helper, p. 29.

tences unpunctuated, all very difficult to read. However, when writing with a sitter, Louisa speaks each word or short phrase (in the case of long words sometimes even each syllable, for example 'e-co-log-ical'), reading aloud as she writes it, so that the sitter can also take it down, which is an asset. Such a method is convincing in so far as there is no idea of the way in which the sentence will work out. However, with time and practice, recently the script has become much clearer to read, with phrases and sentences punctuated. Further, Louisa has grown increasingly aware of perceiving inwardly the concepts presented to her for expression. Indeed as the questions become more penetrating, and the answers (to us) more abstruse, she finds difficulty in doing justice to these ideas and images from the higher worlds for which our limited, materialistic, verbal language is utterly inadequate. Most serious sensitives have this problem; we need an extended language or some more subtle idiom of communication.

Before beginning the writing, there is always a short period of orientation, often combined with healing sent out to the world or to specific individuals in need. When Jessica and Louisa first worked together in this way they used the Invocation; at a certain point Jessica felt it right to change to the Affirmation (of world servers) which we have all now used for several years:

> I am a point of light within a greater Light.
> I am a strand of loving energy within the stream of Love divine.
> I am a spark of sacrificial Fire, focused within the fiery Will of God.
> > And thus I stand.
>
> I am a way by which men may achieve.
> I am a source of strength enabling them to stand.
> I am a beam of light shining upon their way.
> > And thus I stand.
>
> And standing thus, revolve
> And tread this way the ways of men,
> And know the ways of God.
> > And thus I stand.

At the end of the communication we give thanks, close the chakras, and seal our auras and the room with an equal-armed cross within a circle of light.

In 1983 Louisa began to give personal messages to a few carefully selected friends including myself, but since such material is private it is not included here. In almost all cases it was found to be pertinent and helpful. Increasingly, questions were asked on matters of general interest, the replies to which comprise the exercises in Chapter 5. In such a way Louisa found increasing opportunity for informal practice, self-assessment and criticism, also some chance of checking by results. It is not surprising that the early general teachings concerned the nature of guidance and problems associated with increasing psychic and spiritual awareness.

Permeating all the work is the warm and loving nature of Nabraham's communications, often combined with gentle humour. He never hesitates to accept the inevitability of toil and pain in our learning, to give suggestions and even firm advice if asked (for we must always *ask*). But, in referring to us three as his family, he is invariably full of understanding and patience, unfailing and deeply caring love.

An aspect that is not always sufficiently recognised is that the teaching Brothers on the other side need us as much as we need them, for otherwise they cannot reach incarnate humanity. Two years later Nabraham was to say, 'We are nothing without you,' but in May 1983 — a difficult time for me personally — he first put into words the nature of our working relationship:

'Let us take a new look at our friendship. There is now a strong bond. We value the love and offering of your service. We also give you our thanks for the opportunity to be with you. There are many days of bleakness in the life of a human being incarnate. For us the days are a peace and a joy. We do not suffer in the sense that you do. We do, however, suffer from the inability to help with the daily toil. We can watch and guide but cannot remove the burden of just living. We need your help and so we try to lift this for you whenever we can.'

FURTHER TESTS AND ACHIEVEMENTS

In 1982 Louisa had felt mediumship to be her vocation, and in the following year, just as she was about to start in outer life on her university degree course, she made a vow dedicating her life to the path of knowledge and understanding. She wanted to find 'the kind of healing which would restore to the soul of man its original qualities of kindness and love', but the exact form this path would take was as yet unknown. Such a vow almost invariably brings strange changes in consciousness, and, as we all know, self-work is continuous, never finished, so that by early 1985 I felt I must ask Nabraham:

'Could you give us an explanation of what is happening to Louisa? What is she being shown and what is she supposed to be learning?'

He replied, 'Well, it is like the pyramid, this tuning for Louisa. It has been a most painful transition to the next layer of the pyramid which, as you know, contains many passages each of which is a journey in itself, and the knowledge within each journey must be learned.

'This next level contains the messages of the ministers of the world, those who heal and teach.' [To Louisa] 'Your spirit must be scythed before you can reach that level. You are reduced to an infinitely small space before you can enter the narrow portal. Neither pride nor fear nor vanity can enter herein. You are receiving the final steps of disrobement which precede the entry. After this you may be clothed anew in garments of the healing brethren, but for now you must become naked and chaste. This is a preliminary for entry.'

Louisa was about to experience one of those drastically testing experiences of loss that are milestones on the path. I also was just emerging from a kind of bereavement. Nabraham gave encouragement:

'Welcome my friends. We are with you ever in your days: whatever and wherever you are we love and cherish you.

'There is a great sadness at this time, for the end of any relationship is a loss. Whoever goes away is not gone but remains in our hearts. We cannot truly lose those we love for they are in us and are part of what we are. What we can do is to send them along their path with a sure knowledge that we are in them also.

'You cannot let go because you believe that love exists only if you feed it. This is not so. It exists for itself. It is an entity which cannot die but will always be. If you let it go it will not be gone. It *is* you; it is not a thing you can decide upon. Let it be and let it live its own becoming, for there is good to come out of it which shall flower in a new and beautiful land.

'What you can let go of is your own feeling of guilt. You did whatever you could in the circumstances. Do not despair. It is not lost, it is simply going along another path for a time.'

After a few months Louisa had 'made it' to a new, accepting and more objective state of consciousness. Nabraham's response was to some extent a surprise to us in that it showed the degree to which our respective levels of being are so interwoven that our achievements are also theirs.

'There is great joy and peace here today. We bathe in the light of your serenity and we are more happy than you can know, for this trial and this new beginning of a glory is a flame of hope to all who wait in darkness. We stand beside you and are amazed and glorified by your victory. We love and revere you both ever anew, for we are nothing without you.'

There were still inevitable ups and downs. In the autumn, when Louisa was about to start the final year of her course, and I was to undergo an operation for a cataract, Nabraham spoke of our tension and anxiety:

'You are both in a state of expectation and readiness. This creates a degree of tension like the runner waiting for a starter's gun. We understand this and want you to know that there is no need to run the race at all, for we care for and nurture you in every moment. You are protected now as you need so much light to come through this testing time. Both have an endurance test.'

This was followed later by my thankfulness and recognition (yet once again — shall I ever learn?) after a surprisingly easy and successful operation that trust and complete handing over do *work*. Nabraham responded:

'We are blessed indeed by your gratitude. It is for us a joyful sensation to be praised and thanked. We know that you have an inner trust that all is carefully offered up to the plan.'

Then it was Louisa's turn. By January 1986 she had indeed, and most unexpectedly, experienced the 'flowering in a new and beautiful land' (forecast at the depth of her suffering a year before) both outwardly and inwardly. Further, she had now lost the earlier tension and anxiety, being able to 'sit loose' to the thought of final examinations (well achieved in the following June).

I also was feeling a sense of fulfilment, relief at my improved sight, and in particular appreciation of Louisa, Nabraham and his group for their extensive contribution to some research that I had wanted to get into print for twenty years. He thus joined in our celebrations:

'Welcome to you, my own beloved family. We are all together at this time and overjoyed to be with you. There is a time for hard work and a time for joy. This is our joy to be with you when you are so happy. It is a great blessing to have travelled with you through your difficult times and to stand here in the garden of the wilderness where you rest and play awhile.'

AN EXPERIMENT

Over a year later, when Louisa had completed her final examinations and taken a good holiday, the deeper teachings

73

were resumed. Two other factors contributed. First, Louisa's sister Jessica, who had been in close touch with Nabraham throughout her own personal development, now agreed to attempt to channel more general topics. Secondly, some published work of my own, using Nabraham and other sources, had evoked responses in the form of comments and questions which, I felt, might form training exercises for them both. An experienced critic has said, 'In my view the message is as fine as the channel is.' He also stressed the value of dialogue with the teaching guide involving 'answering back'. Therefore, practice in stretching the sensitives' abilities to deal with increasingly difficult topics, including some healthy if nail-biting comparisons between their efforts, seemed useful. The questions were answered separately, neither reading what the other had written until afterwards. Since the sisters share the same guide and teaching group we felt this might be a unique experiment. They live at a considerable distance from one another and differ markedly in personality: Louisa, whose Sun sign is Capricorn, is a self-confessed well-earthed type (see pp. 132–3), while Jessica, an Aquarian, often feels more at home in the inner realms. In Chapter 5 it is interesting to see how similar themes and attitudes vary in approach and detail according to each individual's aptitudes and mental set, albeit showing remarkable consistency and no major contradictions.

Jessica is a qualified yoga teacher with nursing experience and considerable natural healing ability. Recently she has attended some workshops in transpersonal psychology and hopes eventually to train as a counsellor in that field. Her course of therapy with me has lasted for eleven years, involving past-life work, an inner journey and inner spiritual training, with more recent emphasis on implementing the insights gained in outer living.[2]

---

2. See 'The Candle and the Sun', *Light*, Winter 1980.

In the early stages, Jessica had felt and 'seen' Nabraham's form standing beside her, silently and at first indistinctly, while we worked. At the start of her inner journey, again he stood silently, but now with the sun shining through him from behind, simply pointing the way ahead. For a long time she just called him 'my friend'. Later, he began to take a more active part, presenting images and giving short spoken messages. These she heard in her inner ear, repeating them aloud, word by word, for me to take down. Later still, she wrote them herself from inner dictation and in her normal script. Like her sister, however, as she went on she experienced inwardly the presentation of the *whole* meaning (image, concept or idea) then endeavoured to give it consecutive verbal expression. This is shown well in her awareness of the inadequacy of words in the early attempts at replies to far-reaching questions.

Always intensely self-critical, afraid that her own (very active) mind might affect the truth, Jessica had relied for many years on her sister's mediumship — more objective than her own where Jessica's personal material was concerned — and on that of several other psychics. But increasingly Louisa withdrew, feeling that Jessica was well able to use and trust her own, now well-practised gift. Jessica has a strong sense of service, blocked by an equivalently severe lack of confidence in communication. This block has also manifested physically in a syndrome dating from birth; further, we found from our work at a deeper level that it had significant karmic origins running through many lives.

So, in late summer 1986, I asked Nabraham, through both sisters:

'Would you be willing to take part with your group in some research into conditions of being in your world? This would be "research" from our point of view but probably "teaching" from yours; it would help many of us to raise and extend consciousness, possibly developing parts of the brain and nervous system so far relatively undeveloped.'

Nabraham was delighted at this new beginning for the

work, congratulating Jessica on overcoming an age-long block. He told her that although on higher levels the achievement was already won, there would still be a little more physical testing for final clearance (soon confirmed by the last in a series of operations).

'We welcome you into our throng once again. We meet for teaching, for learning, and for loving, as ever. Only trust, for we shall not let you down.'

For Louisa too there was a major break-through. Three weeks before Easter, 1987, Nabraham surprised us by starting the dictation with an invitation to join consciously in their group preparation for the coming festival. We noted the contrast from Septimus' warning before Christmas, 1983 (see p. 68) when guarding the Brothers from our interruptions. But now:

'Welcome to you, my dearly beloved friends. We sit in council today for the beginning of our preparations for Easter. We must become silent and strong together for the giving of light. You may join our efforts every day for a minute, so we can feel your presence among us and be joyous.' This we did.

On Easter Saturday he gave us a special blessing:

'We stand at the altar of life and pray for every soul in torment and every lost lamb who shall be found. We are in the presence of the great masters and we are with you also. This is the trinity of the teaching brethren: the workers on earth, we in the heavens, and the great teachers above even us. We are reverent to our masters and we are joyful that you join in the celebration. Spring overcomes the death of winter and all life is renewed. Spiritual life overcomes the darkness of sad and evil times; so is the cycle of love and purpose entwined and renewed.

'The Lords would that we sit with you in silence for a minute so we can be one.'

(Silence)

'So we rejoice. The final act is achieved. Life transcends

76

death. We are reborn in each other and become as one. The world awaits the final reckoning with the forces of darkness. We have already won the victory, so our work together begins. We set the seal of the Most High upon your endeavours.'

The atmosphere during this communication was so highly charged and beautiful that we found it difficult to come back, feeling greater need than before for sealing and closing down. Louisa sensed that the source was higher than usual. She also had a strong impression of the seasonal significance: that such a ceremony was performed every year, and that although expressed in the Christian idiom of the Resurrection, it was based on much earlier spring festivals.

On a personal level it was probably no accident that from this time Louisa began more direct work as a sensitive. Some years ago, around 1983–4, she had worked anonymously through me as 'postman'. Now she felt ready to sit face to face with a client, or to write personally to those at a distance. She still followed Nabraham's advice (see p. 78): first she dealt with the conscious question, however carefully thought out and framed beforehand; she then encouraged deeper, underlying issues to emerge, allowing plenty of time, and recording Nabraham's responses on each level or topic as it arose. It is a pity that records of such sessions cannot be included here since they illustrate an aspect complementary to the transmission of general information, but for confidential reasons that is not possible. Jessica also has recently embarked on some personal work with some of the same clients as part of the experiment. It is interesting that in certain instances (for example medical matters or causes for handicap) Jessica found her writing change slightly as Nabraham brought in specialists from his group, in one case a doctor, in another someone who had experienced a handicap in incarnate life.

In Chapter 5, however, all messages are transmitted through Louisa unless otherwise stated.

CHAPTER 5

THE EXERCISES

---

*Early Stages: Guides and Systems of Guidance — The Psychic
Levels: Problems Encountered in Spontaneous Psychic
Development — Past Lives and Reincarnation — Group Souls
— Time — The Nature of Soul*

EARLY STAGES: GUIDES AND SYSTEMS OF GUIDANCE

*When Louisa started her work as a sensitive in 1982–3, anony-
mously and through me as link-maker, the requests were all
personal and private. I asked Nabraham how he would like questions prepared and presented.*

Nabraham. What we really need is a simple letter which
gives a little of their history, mostly of family ties and not
necessarily work aspects. Then we would like them to frame
just one question, and this must be very, very carefully
thought about before being written down — at least five or
ten minutes' hard concentration or meditation before the
question is written — for we in fact can find the person by
their thoughts and help them to write down what they
really *need* to know, that is not what they think they *want* to
know!

Q. We have both noticed that you are far more directive in
your messages to Louisa's clients than you were in the
personal teachings given to Jessica, me, and Louisa

herself. Can we ask the reason? Is it perhaps a response to the different kind of questions asked?

Nabraham. We tread carefully where our friends are concerned for we respect their own inner knowledge and know that very direct statements do not help, but concepts and theories can bring them new ideas for their path. With lesser experienced persons we may be more direct, for as yet they have not this ability of working out so intently the meanings behind what we say. We script our messages according to the individual and his ability.

Q. Would you care to comment on the kind of work in this field for which you wish Louisa to be prepared in the future?

Nabraham. There is a general pattern to all this work we undertake in that it involves a feeling relationship that exists between herself and not only us but the persons we help. Those who need help and call to the Brothers of Light are given their help. We answer such calls through a medium sometimes, and this is possible by the medium's own particular way of feeling. Some work through intellect or instinct. For Louisa it is a feeling process and there are no specific people to aim for; they will be brought.

Q. Should we go ahead with this work?

Nabraham. We feel that we will continue to work anyway whatever decisions you take. It is a process of life now and not really a vocation or job to be decided on. Not that there is no choice but that the choice having been made to commit yourselves to the light many years ago, the time now for choosing has long gone.

We did not then foresee that more general questions would be asked. The first set came from a friend:

Q. Do personal guides change as the guided one progresses? For example, a psychically gifted individual

79

may well be aware of many presences around, perhaps helpful but not necessarily of the calibre of the true guide who knows the individual as well as, if not better than, he knows himself.

How then can he find and communicate with his own true guide at the appropriate level?

Nabraham. We would today begin a new idea in the teachings, for these questions are all relevant to the process of individuation.

The acquiring of a guide by an individual incarnate is a long process. It begins before birth and is a process whereby the innate abilities of the individual are assessed before birth by those Brothers who work in the genetic fields. The assessment is of possible abilities, for the reaching up and out to a discarnate guide is not possible for every soul. There is a particular part of the brain which operates this communication. It is developed by the individual through a lifetime, but is almost like an extra finger in that it must be there in order for it to be worked upon. Like the development of any species, this is a slow process; more and more humans have this particular equipment, and many find the way to use it well. Those on the fringes have the dormant part in readiness, but really only personal endeavour can be the operant in making the part work. It is difficult to explain: like having an extra sense that some do not possess at all, but also in that the extra sense is only a potential until it is worked into a talent, the way a musician tunes himself and practises until he is a smooth — that is to say not having blockages — operator.

The guide waits by the souls who do in fact have this innate ability. Many persons see and experience the waiting guide in childhood, but learning obscures this communication. For the naïve or simple, and at the other extreme for the industrious and polished performer, there is a communion of spirit in the making of music. Guidance is a similar occasion. When we discuss this industry, we do not

80

mean that it can be made to happen by constant or impressive work-loads, but that the individual maintains the desire and will to achieve, which brings about the work. This is usually psychological to begin with, in that the person must be freed from his or her life's build-up of negative emotional patterns. This freeing process is long, painful and often depressing, but there are places of light and joy along the way. The more this freeing is done, the nearer to the guide becomes the soul, and communication can begin. There are pitfalls along the way and care and maintenance must be exercised by those in charge of the journeying soul. This is why such persons as Mary are so needed. We need your help to watch and care for our souls in transition.

The journey proceeds and is often more on the level of mysticism and romance, but certain steps have to be taken. These are:

Redemption of one's individual hatred or dislike

Forgiveness of one's persecutors

Acceptance of one's place and of the weakness of others

Dedication to the plan of light, and

Commitment to the work, both on oneself and for others.

Q. What is the structure of the system of guidance from the higher guides' point of view? How is it organised and how are the levels of guidance for incarnates determined? How do guides select the incarnate individual whom they guide?

Nabraham. The guides work with various individuals at many times, but are specific to each in a different way or image, so one guide may have two or three incarnate souls to care for. These groups do not usually meet or know each other, but form a circle of light for the guide's purpose. Those many individuals who do not possess the natural ability to communicate are none the less precious to the Brothers, for they can be unconscious instruments in places, and are even more needful of protection. Like the shepherd and the sheep, we love every sheep and count them all, but those who have this ability are in a way shepherds in the making.

Guides work on a number of themes and belong to different schools, you might say. We in the 'garden' (as we call our Brotherhood) work in the realms of training and understanding and uncovering. It is an intellectual pursuit almost, for we need persons of a certain intelligence to train. Others work in healing. This requires again a different human attribute, that of purity and love. Others work in karmic worlds and scientific endeavours for the advancement of humanity's physical knowledge of itself and the world. There are many groups and many great works.

These Brothers all select their own initiates before birth as I have explained. One could almost say that life really is predestined but only in that one's potential is awaiting the work of training.

But the process of making contact is not easy. Earlier I had asked Nabraham to speak of the different levels of awareness traversed when opening up to guidance.

Nabraham. As you are trapped in your own consciousness, so are we curtailed by it in our ability to make sense for you. You develop slowly and open up a part of yourself that can reach the universal mind. We live daily in this stream of thought; it is our general pattern, but for you it is difficult and strange. By opening up this part you also come into telepathic contact with others of your world who are on this part of the spiral. They unwittingly give out thoughts and you may catch them amongst the rest of your inner vision.

Even more difficult, we found, are those thoughts which invade not from our world but from discarnate sources.

THE PSYCHIC LEVELS:

Problems sometimes encountered in spontaneous psychic development[3]

This dialogue took place during two sessions in July 1983. I had found Wilson Van Dusen's first paper, 'The Presence of Spirits in Madness',[4] to be the most pertinent source of information, but I needed more specific help especially concerning perfectly sane people undergoing spontaneous psychic experiences. Louisa did not read the article until after the first session.

Session 1

Q. An early stage, especially if development occurs fairly suddenly, is that of the 'inane babble' (as Louisa terms it, having once experienced it) or 'Paddington Station' as described by a friend, where the subject is continually invaded by voices.

In his paper, Wilson Van Dusen described some of the more extreme examples from his work in a mental hospital. But it appears that nowadays, in view of the general rapid raising of consciousness, many normal, reasonably balanced people experience this phase, though usually in a less violent or negative way.

In a personal message you did recommend meeting these voices with welcome and tolerance but (as Van Dusen found) they are not amenable to conversation or normal reason; one cannot communicate with them constructively, they just 'keep on'. What to do?

---

3. Subsequently published in *Light*, Winter 1988.

4. *Light*, Summer 1983. Wilson Van Dusen, a psychologist who worked with the mentally ill for seventeen years, researched the inner experience of hallucinations. He describes himself as a phenomenologist, one concerned to discover and describe the real nature of human experience, as was Swedenborg. His published works have interpreted the depths of Swedenborg's findings in terms of modern psychology (see footnote p. 48).

Nabraham. Just as we need to express to you our pleasure in this communication, so indeed do many beings on the astral level need to express their selves to you, that is to those who are newly aware. Thus we may find that a person who begins this work of consciousness-raising will traverse the layers of spirit life.

First, the lower, where may be found those negative, greedy entities who feed upon the material plane and on incarnate persons to give them their sense of being. Those unfortunate enough to encounter this level, as many drug abusers and persons of extremely negative thought-patterns may, are in a sense trapped by these entities, for they do not wish the person to go on and upwards. Great strength and power are needed to remove these entities; often the person himself has not enough power, and help is required.

The less harmful stage of 'inane babble' is above the black pit. It is harmless but irritating for an advanced person to have to go through. Our advice of tolerance and welcome [in a personal message] was in order that no negative steps are made that might precipitate a fall into the 'entity' stage described before. However, we do realise that this level is not helpful or interesting to a person of intellect, but again we must stress that once awareness is opened, it is a stage of spirit that must be traversed. We feel that many can harmlessly await the passing of this stage by tolerance and understanding of these unfortunate persons trapped in the lower astral. Their subjective role is indeed a large part of the individuation process for, however much we might despise and dislike these 'inane babblers', they are in fact a part of ourself, for we have that potential. We are all as bad or as inane as they, at times anyway. So tolerance, we believe, is the key for most normal and ordinarily strong souls.

For those in any danger of falling into madness, there is another way to traverse this stage, and that is denial or denunciation. This may alleviate distressing images but again, on the subjective/objective aspect, nothing exists in the spirit world unless there is space for it in our inner world. Entities that are dark and evil exist, but if in man there were none who had dark and evil places in their own selves then these entities would not be.

Q. A well known medium/psychotherapist recommends exercises with light to clear the aura and the room, dispersing the condition. This worked well in one case. Do you agree?

Nabraham. This is a very positive and useful step to take as long as the light is used in a purposive and unharmful fashion; for these entities in their ignorance should not be harmed, rather helped by a kindly but effective light which does not do any damage to them or to the sender.

Q. Following Swedenborg, Van Dusen distinguishes sharply between what he calls the 'lower order' and the 'higher order' of the true spiritual guides, angels and teachers, who are never invasive. He does not, however, deal with a middle level. Could you please comment on the fact that a person calling for a guide may well be beset by, not evil, but apparently well-meaning spirits who claim to be helpful personal guides yet who are still invasive and, above all, inadequate, giving guidance on a mundane level where it is not required, and failing to understand or give true guidance at the deeper level at which it is needed and requested. Though certainly not 'lower astral', are such voices/spirits from the 'middle astral'? They also do not realise their inadequacy so that efforts to communicate with them are of no use. An experienced spiritual/psychological counsellor has advised telling them firmly to go away, then to try to make contact with the higher guide. What do you suggest?

Nabraham. There is the next level above the 'inane babble' which is more constructive and contains souls who have a great desire to help. Unfortunately, the desire and the ability to help do not always converge, so many on the next level will try to give advice on a number of relatively unimportant issues. Their desire to help is evident; their ability to learn and listen to the person who asks for help is not evident.

This is a guide to their abilities: those who have any approach that invades the one who seeks help are not guides at all but ordinary astral beings who have this unfortunate (for us) desire to help. Once again, to deal with and recognise these entities is the first step; thus again, in a sense, acceptance and tolerance are needed for them to be — that is, to exist. We must not deny them; but to stop their invasion, once again we must be firm yet not unloving in dealing with them. They mean no harm but unfortunately get in the way of many who seek true guidance from their own special source. This is again a stage that will be traversed. Help is at hand, for it is nearer to the guides who can aid a little.

Q. If a person has been advised that his test is 'to distinguish between reality and illusion', this raises the whole issue of the nature of subjective and objective experience. Van Dusen takes the phenomenological approach, i.e. he accepts and deals with what the patient experiences as his own reality. I would like to ask you, from your standpoint, to what extent are these phenomena to be seen as real entities in their own right (for example 'dead' persons inhabiting various levels of the astral plane) or to be understood as constructs of the mind? (I went on to illustrate in some detail the different conceptual frameworks in which they are dealt with, on the one hand as Jungian archetypes and lesser symbolic, subjective images, on the other as seen by clairvoyants objectively as actual obsessing spirits in the aura. This problem was of crucial importance to me, as a psychotherapist, in reference to several cases at the time.)

Nabraham. Ha! This is a test in itself for the person who indeed can distinguish the outer from the inner when the invisible worlds of spirit are in question. Rather, we would like the person to see the test as a test of the ability to *link* the two. Reality is real to the person who experiences. Thus, the phenomenological approach is very good; it gives reality to the person's experience. However, again we feel we must say that the entities and phenomena must exist within the space of the person's self before they can be manifest as an outer or imaged reality. It is not a question really of separating the two but of aligning them, for the one does not exist without the other. Outer reality has no existence without the inner representation. In order to achieve our own individual reality of being, we must deal with this outer/inner question.

Illusion does not exist unless there is a space of madness in the person's self. Madness is where there is extreme conflict, where inner and outer do not align but are in a state of constant battle. The extreme withdrawal and repression of madness is an attempt to quieten the conflict, an attempt to align these worlds. It is in fact an attempt at healing. Withdrawal is a phase of balancing.

The person in question must not be tempted into an intellectual affray with illusion and reality which must be made good friends and aligned, not set against each other.

Session 2

Q. *Regarding those people on the edge of psychosis, in and out of mental hospitals:*

Although (perhaps) not actually possessed by obsessing entities stuck in the aura, they may be pursued by insistent, negative voices telling them (for instance) that they are shortly to die, that there is no hope; they are damned and will go to hell, and often urging suicide.

In my experience, mental hospitals usually offer containment, tests and observation, damping down the symptoms with drugs (which may or may not have side effects) but little more. Many patients are so imprisoned in their fixed, compulsive and repetitive patterns of thought that orthodox psychotherapy and counselling are of no use because they do not touch the patient's perceived reality. There are too few enlightened psychiatrists and psychologists such as Van Dusen who can help them to reach the 'higher order' *in terms of their own experience*. Would you please give advice on the way in which they can be helped?

Nabraham. The mind of the developing soul is like a field that is laid to waste and has become full of weeds and large boulders. Any who come to clearing of the field find a huge task before them. It takes a great dedication to clear and plough the land so that the higher guides can be met. Those who begin must first use great physical effort in order to get the large rocks out. These are the psychological blocks which restrict the mind. There is no short cut to the clearing. It must be undertaken by the souls themselves, and can be aided by helpers on this side.

When the very negative influences abound there is usually a resistance or an inability of the soul to do this work.

There is a way that, in effect, does away with the emphasis on personal blockages. This is to treat the negative voices as small children who are not trained; to speak to them sharply and with great power. This can be done for the soul by one who has strength and power. Like small children, these negative forces will try any trick to get their own way. Like small children they have no real sense of the importance of the other's feelings. That develops from the ability to empathise, which they cannot do. To teach empathy, the child must be given an experience that the other is having; so, to teach these forces to help instead of hinder, they must be trained with a strong and powerful yet kindly hand. Any release from the negative is praised, and praise will also change the children. We realise this is a strange and childish way of treating such demonic-like entities, but in fact it simply *is* the way. They will respond to a stronger voice.

Louisa commented that, as she wrote, she felt that there was no negation of what Nabraham said the previous week about working tolerantly with the less harmful entities. The present script applied to the really harmful ones, not denying them but being very firm.

Q. (by Louisa): The person who can help: is it someone down here or in the other world?

Nabraham. The helper can be a real [incarnate] person who can communicate with these children, if one can be found who has the power and the ability to deal with them. If this cannot be done, then the soul may petition for a [discarnate] helper. We do not give helpers to just anyone, for they are rare and dedicated guides who choose to drop down to this lower level to work. However, through an added dedication to clear the field, the soul may ask for such assistance and it will be given.

Q. Your earlier survey of the lower and middle levels has been very helpful. Could we now go on from there to ask your advice on methods of finding the true spiritual guide? Since, by definition, they are not invasive, they need to be sought and a firm contact gradually and steadily established.

Personally, I was trained through meditation and visual and auditory imagery, with psychotherapy alongside. Of course this method needs a great deal of discrimination since the ego can come in! With some I have used the technique of active imagination as a starting point. Others, on inner journeys, have experienced spontaneous appearances of the true guide at a fairly early stage. Those who are naturally gifted psychically (which I am not) may find the guide through automatic or directed writing, speech, or painting, all of which again need practice and discernment.

I am particularly concerned about ways for those who do not find meditation congenial, yet who are potentially telepathic, clairvoyant and clairaudient, but are still struggling in the middle stage.

Nabraham. The path we take is always a new one for us when we reach out to the higher worlds of the Brothers. Each soul has its own particular type of work and energy. Some are with us in the teaching; some in healing. There are many others, and the way to reach them will differ according to their natures. *We* use insight and understanding, but we can tell of the healing path which uses imagination and imagery.

The work of the Nature Brothers is fairly distinctive and the path thereto is by way of unity with the land, so any who travel this path may find their higher guides in a particular place which fills them with a sense of wonder and awe. Returning often to this place and asking for contact will eventually draw the guide to the soul.

The next step from the middle layer where the helpful, if not too helpful, entities abound is a great step indeed. It is not as quick or simple as the two previous layers for it requires a shedding of the astral layer. This is in fact an initiation which is prepared for carefully by us and will occur at a given time. The soul's work, in order to be ready, is a gradual expanding of insight and understanding of the present life's accomplishment. This takes a fairly heavy toll of souls, for only the very best and strongest can be ruthless with their own self. It requires a complete renewal of attitudes and thought patterns which can be established by reviewing and renewing old stereotyped ways of thinking. This stage is extremely personal and takes a great deal of courage and honesty. It requires that the soul remembers and reviews each stage along the way so far. Attachment to any other soul that stirs any momentous feelings of either dislike or even great love may be that which holds the soul inside the astral plane. To clear these rocks of feeling and thought there must be a dedication to their own soul's release from the karmic ties of this life, which means all must be forgiven and all must be praised in the name of the Self or the God Within who can only be released from the astral chains if each chain is carefully untied.

As she wrote, Louisa felt the meaning of Nabraham's theme was that it doesn't all have to be done from the ego; it is the dedication to the work that matters. Once you get to that point, the guide can reach you. She said, 'There is the image of a locked door with a keyhole. They are waiting on the other side, calling, but we have to turn the key. The key is acceptance and responsibility for one's life as it is, with no "if only" or blaming circumstances, and then willingness to change.'

PAST LIVES AND REINCARNATION

The need for self-work is clear, but how can this best be done? As well as learning from daily living and perhaps from conventional psychotherapy, to what extent is the recall of past lives useful? In 1985 Nabraham agreed to give his views to help me with a paper on the subject,[5] saying that the Brothers in his teaching group were already pooling their ideas to assist my understanding.

Nabraham. There are many ways to uncover the nature of our here-and-now problems. Past-life work is a unique way. The nature of the person will dictate how it should be done.

For the concrete reality-based person — that is one who cannot take flight in realms of vision — the best procedures are by relating to facts of the day and by uncovering illusory thoughts which stem from guilt, sorrow and loss. These are anchored in the reality of people and relationship. The way to cure the problem is by changing the personal way of dealing with people.

The majority of those we meet are worldly and do not relate to other spheres. But those who are not so fond of the reality of the concrete world — that is those not tied down by sensation and thought — can choose a multitude of ways

---

5. *Light*, Spring 1986.

to deal with problems, in fact many of their problems are due to this other-worldliness. By relating to an inner world we transcend the difficulties we have with people. So meditation, religion and occult science *can* all take us away from those insidious persons who would bring us back to the reality which we do not like.

Past-life redemption is another such method. It is more personal and reality-based because it involves the individual and others who are known; thus there is a link with reality. This link is both a helpful and a hindering factor. It makes sense that those we encountered in other times are those we suffer with now. This anchors reality and is beneficial, yet also it disclaims to a degree the responsibility of doing here and now what is necessary to resolve the problem. But if the person can take their visions and bring them into the present (by an act of faith almost) and give of themselves what is needed, which may be forgiveness or even ruthless cunning — the list is almost endless for each situation requires its own solution — then to be sure reality-based solutions will occur. We can use these past-life visits to apply the knowledge *now*, for in the final reckoning it is only and always NOW that karma is resolved.

Karma itself is not an objective fact; it is an inner subjective reality which is felt and experienced.

Louisa sensed that Nabraham was trying to convey the idea that negative karma exists in so far as we experience such happenings with guilt. The important factor is the feeling we have about them, the feeling changing as our consciousness of the world changes. For example, an action in one century and place may be felt as bad, in another as not wrong. Nabraham continued:

Nabraham. Thus we find that we are overloaded when we take in and take on much of the human situation that we truly do not own, and yet it is ours by birthright. In that I mean that those who bear us pass on their problems, guilt and unfulfilled expectations. We take on this burden and by so doing make it our own. This is very necessary, for progress cannot be made unless the past is redeemed by us.

Q. A therapist experienced in past-life work has commented, 'An important theoretical point I find is to help the present incarnate personality to disidentify from the one that is being investigated, and see the redemptive task, thus releasing guilt.' Do you agree?

Nabraham. Yes, this is of great importance. If the person can see the problem as a situation rather than as an involvement, that is to say be objective about the vision, he can gather the knowledge which it offers and see it for himself. So, when a past life is seen not only as personal but as a story with a moral — or more a key or clue to what happens now — then the energy for the work is available. If the person lays emphasis on personal guilt and redemption of personal sin, then the work now is hindered. But the link must be retained; the link is the knowledge.

Q. In past-life work, to what extent is suffering inevitable?

Nabraham. The function of suffering is to bring the person to a point of wanting more than anything else to get a solution, to take on the problem for the self rather than to see it outside in the world. Suffering is not absolutely necessary as such, but it certainly speeds the process of resolution, for when we are comfortable we often do not seek the answers.

Q. How does this apply to X (someone who felt far more at home in the inner, ideal worlds)?

Nabraham. Her suffering is a kind of bleak, unknowing, non reality-based quest for the solution. It teaches her again to look into her own way of dealing with the world. It is an extremely unpleasant suffering which teaches her to modify her own view of the truth, for even the limited, reality-based people have their right to their own kind of truth. She somewhat denies them this and, in a way, acts as foolishly as do they when they deny her inner reality.

Q. Can we, as Seth suggests, speaking through Jane Roberts, change the so-called past and even the so-called future?

Nabraham. The actions of the past as you see them are unchangeable in their form, but they are extremely mutable in their meaning, and it is the meaning of the past that is your only real history. As such, you can in many ways change what has happened, so by reliving and reinterpreting the past you do in fact change it, for its only reality in the now is what traces are left in the psychic life of those involved. Thus you change yourself by relinquishing the actions of the past through your own intuition. By this work the future also is changed, for actions of the future proceed from the meaning of the past. Thus past and future exist only in the reality of *now* and in the meaning given to them by the self.

Q. Does the frequency of incarnation vary with the age of the soul, as some would suggest? For instance, do young souls reincarnate more frequently, older souls taking more time in the higher worlds to consolidate and distil the essence of their previous life's experience between incarnations?

Nabraham. There exists a formula, almost, for the relationship of returning to an earthly body. It is something of a paradox, for those who do little while they live will be required to do much whilst they return after death. In a sense they must release energy for rebirth. When a soul comes back who has achieved some express task, it will be given more time to retrain its family. We are struggling to disentangle the individual lifetime of a soul from the many lives of its family of souls. There is in a way no unique lifetime or soul, for each is enmeshed in the one life and knowledge pool. But individuals do vary in their skills and some may take on the burden of many lives quickly in order to fulfil some plan of the group. So you see it cannot quite be stated that this happens *or* that, for the formula is a whole pattern consisting of many, many points of light which change continually, each having some moment of brilliance and then returning to daily ordinariness.

Q. I have two friends (each working with other therapists) who have apparently incarnated very rapidly after the last war having purportedly died in Jewish concentration camps. Can you comment?

Nabraham. There is always a great need for the soul who passes in torment to return, so that this is allowed even though the next life is uncomfortable, for the aftermath of such a horror as the last war is a time of great awareness. Humans are integrating this terrible experience, and the souls who most need to come to terms with that horror can benefit from being alive during this after-war transition stage. They can learn to alter their own feelings as they grieve for and diminish their own deaths.

These preliminary teachings, circulated to a few interested readers, provoked considerable correspondence.

Q. (from an applied mathematician with a special interest in reincarnation). World population today is $4\frac{1}{2}$ billion and by the end of the century, provided we avoid a holocaust, will be at least six billion. Demographers tell us that world population BC never exceeded 200 million *at most*. If six billion units (let alone the sixty billion referred to by H.P. Blavatsky and Alice Bailey) are seeking experience in physical incarnation, but there are, at most, only 200 million physical bodies available, the *average* inter-incarnation period becomes very large. What is the explanation? I feel that somewhere there is a factor missing. For any comments I should be most grateful, as it is a question I am naturally and invariably asked whenever I talk about reincarnation.

Nabraham. (through Jessica — her earliest attempt at this work).

We will try to be simple in this, for to know in detail will not help those who have not the eyes to see or the eye of understanding. To 'see', we would need to tear the scales from the eyes. Shall we say it this way?

There are tides and seasons, as you know, and [chuckle] the number of souls waiting to incarnate as you suggest conjures up a picture which is quite funny really, for there are not queues of people as you imagine waiting in line for incarnation. The vastness of what you call space *is* vaster than you can imagine and not one is idle in their wait, for experience goes on at all levels, at all times, and the experiencing takes place in many and varied places. When we say 'places' it is for your understanding (which is limited while looking through the physical senses). The mind is the tool of the spirit, but unfortunately the mind has taken the dominant position, and until men can look through the eye of the spirit instead of the eye of the mind, comprehension will be limited. The mind sees all in duality; the spirit sees differently. It is much the same with all things in the manifest plane. All is seen in terms of opposites, whereas the reality of spirit is the unmanifest.

Jessica was quite unhappy about this first effort; she felt it was so general that it did not properly answer the question and might only confuse further those who had originally raised the subject at lectures. So I (Mary) asked the following:

Q. Could you please, as a teacher, make a bridge to the earth-bound mind and give the kind of explanation that might help to 'open the eye' of the questioner? For example, could these 'places', in part, be on other planets?

Nabraham. Look upon this planet earth as a schoolroom for it is truly a place of learning. What you ask about other planets is true, for there are 'places' which are not schoolrooms but places of real work and putting into practice all that has been gained on planet earth. Therefore to see

96

queues of people waiting to incarnate on the earth is really not to understand the reality of incarnation.

The fullness of growth on the earth becomes a fully conscious manifestation of the spirit whereby a soul passes on to other conditions of growth and maturity. It is far better to know and learn of what one needs — to become perfected in one's own sphere — than to try to encompass conditions which are out of reach for you. In the full maturing of the consciousness all becomes clear; the eye of the spirit is then automatically opened and truth is seen *as it is*.

Q (Mary). Thank you. I now refer back to the opening statement of the question illustrating the immensely rapid increase of present population compared with the maximum of 200 million BC. Would you please comment on the reason for this? Are more souls needing experience nowadays in the schoolroom of planet earth?

Nabraham. We will try again to put this in the context of tides and seasons for your understanding.

As you know, on earth you have seasons where in spring everything begins to grow; in summer all is profusion and nature flourishes in gay abandon — there is much growth and overpopulation of things. Then in autumn everything begins to grow weaker and to fade; whilst in winter everything dies in order to be reborn in spring — the ever-returning circle. Looked at in this way perhaps we can see that the earth and all the vastness of space (as you call it), encompassing many, many other planets, has an even larger circle of return. So you see that the population of the earth reaches full proliferation now, and as in many other times there is a winter when a clearing out (so to speak) is done and the cycle begins again. Think of the many stories where people were destroyed in the floods but yet a few were saved wherewith to begin again the cycle. But look not upon all those destroyed as lost, for as in nature nothing is really lost but merely continues in another form.

Q (Mary). Would you mind my asking the same question through Louisa, for the sake of the experiment?

Nabraham. Do go ahead, Mary. Our blessings go with you as always.

Nabraham. (*through Louisa*). The question: well, the mathematics do not add, as the gentleman can see. However, there is not a simple one-to-one relationship of body and soul. As it were, the group soul contains the embryos of multitudes of living persons, but only one or two of each group or family ever incarnate together. Experience of these explorers in the flesh is gained by the whole group, so number counts are not terribly important, but ability to communicate — to be in touch — with the incarnate soul *is* important.

Originally, only the leader or initial soul members incarnated. They learned and grew and passed on this knowledge to their group. As population expands, more of the group can incarnate together, but there are always embryos awaiting in the soul world, as in the flesh. Neither we nor you can truly understand infinity or eternity, yet we are attempting to compress these terms into head-counts. Souls are numberless and so there will always be a circle or cycle of birth and death. As below, so in the upper realms souls grow older and reunite with the great Infinite. While there are new souls becoming, the wisdom of the older souls is passed on just as it is on earth. We cannot begin to speak in terms of time and number as they do not exist here really. All that exists are the bonds within and between soul groups.

Q. (Mary — trying desperately to get some more tangible reply to send to the questioner). Would you please say more about the inter-incarnational period as emphasised in the question?

Nabraham. The fact that some souls remember several incarnations during periods of only a few years, and yet there are

98

obviously not enough bodies for all the souls waiting, is explained by the joint experience of a soul group. What one individual experiences becomes the life-memory of the whole group, so individuals remember four or five lives which belong to the whole group, not to the individual personality. Once this one-to-one relationship of life and soul experience is discounted, the time between experiences or lives ceases to be any sensible question. You can live three lives without incarnating, as your soul group members have done it for you. Simply, we are trying to say that each lifetime becomes individual *and* group experience, regardless of which personality lived the life.

The correspondent, realising that the wrong question had been asked, still maintained that the rapid increase in world population does constitute a major stumbling block for those beginning to take reincarnation seriously. About the concept of group souls he kept an open mind. Another reader told us that her father, a theosophist, had commented through a medium after his death that the lectures he had given on reincarnation during his lifetime were misleading. He now found the whole phenomenon to be far more complicated than he had realised. With this finding we all profoundly agreed.

GROUP SOULS

The need to extend our present conceptual framework was becoming increasingly obvious. One way was by further dialogues to attempt some degree of imaginative comprehension of the many-dimensional nature of individual and group existence.

Q. On the theory of group souls, we are told that we incarnate in soul groups, interacting with members of that group, life after life, working out karma for the whole. How much are we working for ourselves, for those of our incarnate group, for the general group soul, and for more extensive racial and cosmic levels?

Nabraham. Surely and safely we are trying to lead you to an understanding of that which is almost not within your reach. There are families of souls which you might call a group soul whose members are finely attuned to each other. As in any family they come together often during an age, some incarnate whilst others remain to watch over and guide and also to learn from [incarnate] life. Thus, any life-lessons are never just for the individual but are much wider than this. For what happens to one in a family happens to all who share their link. So we have families of souls and members who all belong to a group. It will be a large group of some several hundred souls. Alongside these families are the greater group levels. We have perhaps six or seven in this country along the lines of racial belonging. We can interchange our race from time to time as lessons for the others [i.e. to feed in that particular experience], so we gain knowledge of all groups.

Q. According to one authority, it follows that it is possible to blend in thought with the memories of those who are akin to our soul. So, not all far memory may be from our own individual reincarnation. Please comment.

Nabraham. Family links mean that any incarnate has the knowledge of all his family at his finger tips and can dip into it as into a book of knowledge. Thus we may see ourselves as victim in a life yet in fact we may have been a bystander in that scene. It is very important to *know* when an act has harmed. We are responsible for all acts within our family and so the scene is real, even if we individually were not victim or agent. For we are not simply a part of each member but irreplaceably one and the same.

Louisa felt the idea was this: as a bystander we may not have realised the harm, so we are allowed to go back and be the victim in order to understand it.

Q. Then this eliminates so much *personal* guilt?

100

Nabraham. We are the representative of all of the family, and thus we are the sum total of everything the family has done or been.

We find that there is difficulty with words today, but this might help. Those in the body are the representatives of the greater numbers of the family, just as politicians represent their constituencies. Their acts affect and represent the whole, so they have much responsibility and much left-over guilt to deal with, but can stand aside from personal blame, for they are mainly trying to resolve and improve what has gone before.

These concepts provoked considerable discussion and questions from readers.

Q. Are all the souls in a group soul on the same level? If not, how does a group soul work if parts are on different levels? And if they are on the same level surely some of the souls amongst the group souls are more experienced than others?

Nabraham. We are well pleased in the responses to our message. It is difficult to express how complex and yet how simple the group soul is. Liken it to a man who has many separate cells, many distinct organs, and yet is a united integrated whole. A soul group contains members on different levels such as the hands, feet, and brain which are certainly at different levels of organisation and importance. However, all levels interact, and many cells can do the work of others when necessary. Injury to one part of the structure will be known by all other parts as in negative karma which is an injury to the group. Thus injury to the hand may require the help of many other parts of the body for healing. The group soul is a wholeness. While individuals remain distinct they do have an integrated memory and can take over the work for other parts. An example of this would be in skin-grafting where one area can replace another. Also geneticists now realise that developmentally cells can produce the correct pattern when displaced. Thus it is a pattern

101

or a plan of the group hierarchy which differentiates individuals into higher or lower, rather than any individual knowledge.

Although still lacking in confidence, for the sake of the experiment Jessica also had a go.

Nabraham (through Jessica). In order to answer this question in depth one must go into a study of vibrations, for levels are one but vibrations or frequencies are many. What the questioner asks can best be answered by an illustration.

The members of a group or family exist as that group or family by the correspondence of their vibratory note or key. Thus, according to their vibratory note they will be attuned to each other. In this way we have similarity of endeavour and purpose in the divine plan. We may say that among the group family we will have some souls on the earth level, in incarnation, working within the limitations of the physical vehicle, but yet their souls will be attuned to the note of the group. This is why attunement to the soul is first required, for only through the soul can one's group family and its purpose be contacted. We then have members of the family working on other levels, and in this way a chain is formed, and always the linking is the note or key. Many of the family do not know, or are not aware of, their family group as yet, but still they work on ever according to the plan, for always a brother of more advanced stature walks with the brother who is not yet aware, and in this way guides and directs his brother's steps. Ever the way is by gentle guidance and steering in a certain direction. Of course the free will of the brother is preserved, but then free will itself needs to be understood more deeply, for until a soul is free there is very little free will *per se*.

Yes, some of the group *are* more experienced than others, and it is the wish and the duty of the more experienced to teach and guide their younger brothers, leading them ever onward to greater recognition of the purpose and plan of their group. For as purpose and plan become more con-

102

scious in the mind of a brother, his work and service become more consciously directed and sure.

Q. When discussing reincarnation [see pp. 94–5] you mentioned that a soul who has achieved some express task will be given more time after death 'to retrain its family'. Please enlarge on this.

Nabraham. The retraining of the family is hard to express for your understanding in a few words, but it is rather like sending a child to school, and upon his return he shares his knowledge with the family. It may be that the rest of the family are elsewhere, learning other aspects of wisdom, and then it is all shared. Remember that soul is *one* and that if viewed from this oneness then individuals as such do not exist. Can you grasp this concept? For this is what we mean by being difficult to give you understanding in words, for soul and soul levels are all one.

Here Jessica had an image of a hand pointing downwards. The fingers represented individuals in incarnation transmitting their experience to the palm, the soul.

Q. They talked of work they did between coming together as a group. What work is this? At one point [see p. 111] he says love is work. Would this be work for the individual soul or group soul?

Nabraham (through Louisa). Well, the work can be anything at all really, perhaps watching over loved ones who are close to the discarnate, perhaps teaching younger souls, perhaps healing work. Really there is as much to do in our world as there is in yours, so we are busy people; and yet our work is mostly quietly sitting beside those who are struggling to understand and grow. Work is chosen so that each individual soul can grasp and integrate the previous lifetime. After completion of this task, more expansive work can be done.

Nabraham (through Jessica). We have our separate work and

103

our group work where we come together. However, the work is one work. It is only that we each have a younger brother in our keeping and sometimes several brothers, according to our specific learnings and preferences in the work. Some work more on the line of healing, where others lean more to teaching. Therefore, our combined work is a pooling of specific 'talents', as you would call them. Just as you have specialists in medicine, law and physics, etc., we too have members who have specialised more in any one way or another. And so if a brother has under his wing a brother in the flesh who is involved in medicine and following that line of development, then the brother here will also have followed that line of development. In this way we have a greater facility in attunement and the bringing together of souls within a group. The point to remember is that it is the vibration of the soul which brings group families together and enables them to influence and *be* influenced or guided.

Your final point about love being work may be stated also the other way round, for to work is to love. Seen from our viewpoint then, love is work and work is love. This work and this love, being the same thing, is ever for the good of the whole, and although at times especial effort be made on behalf of one aspiring individual, this is only a part of a greater effort for the whole group.

May we conclude our session with a thank you and a blessing, for we welcome these communications and trust always that they serve for greater understanding, widening and broadening of the view-point.

With love and blessings we depart with joy. Peace unto you.

The next set of questions from readers involved the possibility of higher animals evolving and incarnating into the human life-stream. Louisa, who transmitted the first answer, was surprised at it, explaining that in view of her biological training and her love of animals she had thought there was an evolutionary transition between animals and mankind. So here is an example of the teaching being in complete contradiction to the sensitive's beliefs.

Nabraham. The animal kingdom is a separate world entirely from the one we inhabit. They have only to become close to humans and they graduate to a kind of astral world where they are available to humans. Such a love relationship enlarges the soul of the animal and it progresses through a series of lives whereby it can become a human aid. There is never a full transition to the state of humanity, for animals remain animals but do progress in knowledge to a certain point. The group soul enlarges with the individual experience, thus pets obviously come high among the animal kingdom, and many pets such as dogs, cats, and horses do join the middle worlds where they remain as servants and lovers for human kind.

Q. (Mary). Please define 'middle worlds'.

Nabraham. This area is likened to our astral plane and we can meet the animals here. For them it is their highest realm, so the individual animal has here reached its ultimate goal.

One questioner, while accepting that each animal has its group soul from which individualisation of some higher mammals can take place to a degree, then applied the concept to humans. (He had read much of Steiner and similar authorities.)

Q. Does the human group soul evolve and individualise in a similar way, for example, when unevolved but emerging individuals, having a common karma, gain from the experience of those which incarnate? Then, when more evolved, the separate human individual souls would produce facets, each of which can incarnate with a personality of its own, one facet or more at a time, this being part of its experience? If so, each individual soul would then have its own karma as well as group karma, race karma, and world karma.

Nabraham. We find it difficult to give a rational explanation as all is eternal, and so to describe a beginning is not so easy. However, in time long ago man became aware of himself as a creature whose death might come at any moment. This awareness was the key to karmic ties, for only in a world of ending and beginning can karma operate. Thus the soul is tied to the body only whilst death is seen as an end to him- or herself.

Soul groups have always existed and evolved; in our world there are those who have not yet incarnated and those who have done so. The individual soul experiences its group's growth and evolution. However, once incarnate, that soul makes deeper relationships to others. This is the essence of karma. In a sense it depends upon our love ties and upon our emotional dependencies. Karmic life has a momentum which impels us to reparation, and the group will share each individual's work-load.

The idea of facets of a person's existence we do not support. The whole soul incarnates otherwise there would not be the dedication and searching which incarnates suffer to right a wrong. The link with our world is the ties to the group, so an individual might sense himself as not wholly part of the incarnate world because his ties are so intimate with souls in this world. The chains of togetherness are bound about us in such a way that the two worlds are meshed by love and memory.

Defining 'facets' more exactly, the questioner persisted.

Q. I think that each individual must be responsible for his own karma, but perhaps is able to gain from the experience of the various facets [personalities] which the soul puts down on earth for experience, perhaps more than one at a time. I feel that the human evolution has evolved individuals from a group, from a long way back, but that the group still persists as a group of individuals, linked of course, but still individuals.

Nabraham. Individuals in no way lose their personal karma

106

even though the group can alternate and work with them on this karma, for knowledge and experience of the group are enhanced when many come together to learn the wisdom of such karmic lives. However, the individual becomes emotionally bound by the karma. His or her soul companions are like agents or representatives who can take on some aspects of the working through. Thus the members of the group are interchangeable and yet each retains a personal karma by their ties to the individual with whom the karma operates.

As to the facets of a soul, we see it operates less precisely than this, for a soul will choose parents and conditions which provide a basis for life experience. From this is the personality built each time the individual incarnates. However, each personality will merge with the soul radiance and this has no specific personality or personalities. It is simply an expression of the group work, i.e. some are teachers and some healers, etc.

The personality is influenced by the soul and this, in a sense, is some of the purposes of incarnation: that the given personality created by genetics and conditioning be gradually modified by the soul's radiance. Thus the soul forms and informs the personality.

Increasingly we realised that we could not conceive of the interaction between timebound individuals and timeless soul groups without more study of the meaning of time.

Nabraham. When you want to think about time and groups, you cannot really grasp that time does not exist in days or even years, but it exists in learning and accomplishment. We progress, not in time, but in knowledge, so from where we are, time is an illusion. Yet it is a real thing, for you face your own death and this is the only reason that time is so difficult for you. If you had no image of the end of a life, then you would not hurry to learn; you might become indolent and believe that it is not important to strive for knowledge. There is a real need to have a time limit, for as in a classroom the sound of a bell means that what is not done must be accomplished another day. Do you see that it is important to maintain belief in time limits?

And again:

Nabraham. We are strong and glad today, for even though you weary a little, you are both on the brink of new and exciting times. This leads into the subject, for I say to you 'new times' as if it were a different day or a different hour. Even so, you will see that time, as such, is not measured by the glass but by the experiences of life. You may live one hundred years and still we only see your life as a progression of experience and knowledge. If you learn from this experience you truly live in time, but if you do not, time stands still.

TIME

At quite an early stage (January 1984) Louisa had an intensely vivid dream in which she was shown with demonstrations that time and space do not exist in the higher worlds. She herself asked Nabraham for help.

Q. If time and space do not exist, then we do not live from day to day but from one big moment to another, from happening to happening. Certain incidents in life are meaningful. If that is so, how do I cope with my daily life which I find so constricting? How can I get through time?

Nabraham. Come to us, for this is a question that has ever been in the mouth of man. How indeed to toil and labour when there is no fruit and no joy in the work?

We cannot explain the intricacies of time, but it really is an illusion. If you can, even for a moment, feel the eternal nature of your real self, then you can live in time, for it is nothing to the timeless soul which views the day as an opportunity for love. A soul is a being of extreme patience and does not feel the irritations of the personality which is the part that struggles in the world of time. You can be in touch with this eternal truth at all times, but it requires a shift of consciousness into the 'now' which all great teachings emphasise. Living in the moment is difficult. It takes a loss of personality and goals. You need to be utterly flexible and without greed, for only the greedy live towards the next day, when 'now' is all we can really own.

We do not explain this well; indeed it cannot be an understanding; it requires an insight or intuition. This can best be accomplished by taking every incident every day and every moment as a gift.

We long for incarnation so that we may give back all the glorious experience we have, but it is not so for us. We cannot return; we can only give this to you. We would like to thank you for your efforts and inspirations to others. This is our only gift to others.

We discussed greed. While admitting that it was the cause of much of the world's inequalities and wars, we suggested that on a personal level a major factor in being unable to live in the moment was anxiety. Certain messages from discarnate sources other than Nabraham were creating great anxiety about the future.

Nabraham. We do understand the anxiety of such messages. Living under them has created a tense and irritable manner which we see by the loss of a certain sensitivity. The purpose is that we must not expect; we must not plan; we must not fix for ourselves some future point at which we can be happy. To be happy is also an illusion that time creates. Happiness is not in conditions; it is an attitude towards all conditions, a long and bitter lesson but all that is learned will be fruitful, for the life of our friends is never one of ease. You need extremes of strength and endurance beyond the normal. We have created conditions for you to experience strengthening, and now you can survive anything of the world.

Louisa explained that by 'friends' he meant 'those on the path'. During the next few years she herself was to experience the further severe testing already described — and more.

Two years later my second, more theoretical, paper on 'Psychotherapy and Past Lives'[6] started an 'Ongoing Discussion'[7] mainly concerning our changing perception of time beyond the linear concept experienced in our incarnate space/time continuum.

Nabraham (through Jessica). On this we could write a book, for to your understanding it is very complex. Not complex of course to us who stand this side, but complex to the limited tool, the mind. The necessary deeper realisation entails a wider consciousness. However, we will try to put it into some order for your comprehension.

Try to see death as a birth, a beginning instead of an ending. In this way it is better understood, for when first born into new surroundings and new landscapes there is a necessary period of disorientation until the soul is aware of the new environment. Time as such does not exist at this stage. Much like a new-born baby: time does not exist for a baby, time is merely dictated by the bodily needs such as hunger, discomfort and so on. It is much the same with a soul being born to the other side of the veil which you call death. At a later stage, the soul becomes more and more awake in its new surroundings and aware of other souls in its vicinity.

Now, the soul is born into those conditions and surroundings which befit the state of consciousness and its stage of growth. Therefore, the environment will be peopled by those of similar nature, tastes, desires and states of being. There will always be some souls to meet the newly arrived, and in this way help is provided for the new soul to adjust.

There are stages which one passes through and at each

---

6. *Light*, Spring 1986.

7. *Light*, Autumn 1986, Spring and Winter 1987, and Spring 1988.

stage time as such differs. For on other planes the states of consciousness differ, and with ever-expanding consciousness time becomes increasingly flowing and moves into the all — Now — the is-ness, the be-ness, of eternity.

Q (Mary). Could you please concentrate on the differing sense of time at each level? For example, a questioner wants to know how the inhabitants of each level organise their communication and social life which on this earth we do by making appointments.

Nabraham. Time is structured here by one's work, and work is not work as you know it, for to love here is to work, and time as such does not enter in. If we should wish to communicate we merely need to think of the person and we are instantly in rapport. All is done differently and there is not the need of arranging as you call it. Also, to communicate with anyone on one's own level of consciousness is all so simple. The difference is in communicating with one on another level, and here it is best to use the analogy of Jacob's ladder, for we need our intermediaries to facilitate the communication, rather like you have interpreters on the physical plane.

At this point, Jessica felt that words were so inadequate that she was actually holding up the transmission by trying to use them. She received the whole concept in images, by-passing her intellect.

Jessica. I see a picture of souls, beings, who are like invisible energy structures, whose 'bodies' are a pulsating, flowing mass of forces and currents which register every vibration. It is rather like our radio and television waves; we do not see them but yet the pictures and words are *there* all the time; we merely need to press a button to receive. What I see is the same on the other side. Without the gross physical body a soul is like a receiver and a transmitter, and it is only the limited human mind which blocks out the signals, impulses and messages which are here and now all the time.

The same question was put to Louisa.

Nabraham (through Louisa). In our world there are several layers of functioning. Those who are most involved in the teaching aspect operate on your own time dimension as well as by the other dimension; that is, they are aware and tuned in to the day/night rhythms in order to be available and useful to incarnates. The other time function is a sensory process of the mind rather than the body.

We are tuned to the leader or key figure of our group. He will let us know at all times when and where to meet, so for this meeting I have called together some twenty souls who sit with me in the communication. We are all able to communicate individually to each other merely by directing the mind towards an individual. So time is unnecessary owing to the fact that place and space hold no hindrances to our communication. Do you see how time and space interact in your world to make it necessary for sensory physical time, while here there is no need for either? However, in order to co-ordinate our actions (which are the only reality here, action being thought usually) we need to be in constant communication with our group via our group leader who is controller of our operations. He will call us as a church bell calls you to service. Upon the call, which is a thought message, we know there is work to be done or a need for group counsel. In such a way are our lives ordered. We go about our personal work and simply tune in occasionally to each other. When necessary, each of us can call a meeting. We do not even need to be all together for group counsel, but it is a more powerful process if we do sit together in space. Thus, simply, our time-sense derives from our non-individuality in thought and is ordered by our work and group needs.

Q (Mary). Thank you. That is a perfect description of the way an evolved group, dedicated to teaching, functions. Could you please speak of individual souls who perhaps have only recently passed on?

Nabraham (through Jessica). The physical needs do not completely disappear when rebirth happens [i.e. birth into after-death conditions]. It is all according to the stage and state of the passing soul. The varying degrees of awareness or awakeness actually dictate the needs of the soul. In this way, each is born into its appropriate surroundings and therefore there is no *one* answer to this question. For the various levels have their own operations according to the consciousness of the inhabitants.

Of course the needs change according to the stature and maturity of the soul; therefore one who has gone beyond needs of the physical body is born into higher levels of comprehension, and hence the needs become even higher, although to say higher we do not mean to imply anything superior. For what one eats as a baby cannot be called inferior, can it? Merely right for its stage of growth. It is much the same with this question; needs change as consciousness expands, and therefore the needs become ever more subtle and leave the gross behind.

The questioner herself offered the following explanation:

Q. I think the mind, as a 'body', makes temporal patterns of some sort just as the physical body does. Which means that we must distinguish between the mind as an energy structure, and consciousness as that which experiences through this structure. The mental time of discarnates could very well order past, present and future very differently from the body's physical time.

Nabraham (through Louisa). The mind is tuned via the etheric body of the old brain-stem part of the brain. This is the old animal brain which perfectly picks up the minute signals of seasonal changes and earthly signs of time. So the new soul will have a greater need and therefore a greater ease of remaining earthbound in time. However, he or she will also have 'communication time sense' via the pineal gland of the brain. These structures interact beautifully in our world,

113

and are evolved only in special or specific persons in your world. Death changes nothing in the sense that the etheric brain still operates in the etheric body. The energy of memory is the strongest time sense we have until all those we specially love pass over. Then we begin the work of the soul life. The [etheric] brain loses its need for memory time and becomes more truly non-timebound and eternal. Past and future are terms which we use only of experience and not of moments. The structure you experience by is the physical brain, and at the same time that experience becomes independent of the physical brain structure, passing into the etheric brain. The memories live as experience or knowledge through the etheric body.

We can try to explain this by drawing an analogy with a painter who paints a picture which exists in time and space. Thus he has created the finite evidence of his mind-energy. The world is the picture and those incarnate are the brush strokes which do exist in their own time and place. Were the picture to be erased, it would not leave a blank space; having existed it remains both in the mind of the painter and of those who have witnessed it, and also it remains upon the canvas, however lightly it remains.

Here Louisa also felt words to be less meaningful than the inner image. She sensed that even if it were scrubbed with biological washing powder the canvas would retain the 'memory', and that we could revive it if only we knew how. The concept of the Akashic records came into her mind, and the impression of everything having its etheric replica.

When all this material had been sent to the questioner, she replied that what specifically concerned her was not so much how the dead communicate with the living but how they relate to one another without invasion.

Q. Not all discarnates are involved in service to incarnates and I am sure they need some privacy in the beyond as we do here. One would need the protection of some sort of spiritual answering machine if people can contact one

114

merely by 'thinking at one'.

Louisa being abroad, Jessica agreed to have a shot at a reply.

Nabraham (through Jessica). In the previous answers we were talking of the work which groups do who are committed and dedicated to the helping and serving of those aspiring souls on earth, and to group service in world affairs.

It would help the lady if she were to take the earthly set up as an example. Many people work and live and love for themselves, their own little families and affairs, do they not? These people are only concerned with small matters such as food and warmth, shelter and so on. They have neither the awareness nor the inclination to be working for anything higher or deeper. In so being, they are not able to receive anything higher and they remain on this level for many lives.

There is this same development as you travel the levels, and here there are many who do not have the spiritual equipment of which we have talked in order to communicate and receive communication. It is only as a soul develops that he or she is enabled to receive and relay teachings or other services. And in this development of the equipment we do have the 'spiritual answering 'phone' that you speak of; this may surprise you, but there are many things which you are unable to imagine as yet, but only wonder at.

Nabraham then showed that there was no need for individual privacy at his own level. This is reminiscent of many wise teachers who, after death, reassured their former pupils that they were not 'bothered' by being called upon for help, e.g. Andrew Glasewski who is reported to have explained, 'I am a thousand Andrews'. Nabraham continued:

There is no need for protection, for our equipment is for the purpose of being of service wherever there is a need. And, in order to be of use in whatever way is needed, our attuning instrument is open at both ends. It is difficult to explain in terms of your understanding, but try to imagine it

115

as a switchboard with many lines, and because the sensitivity and awareness are not boxed in as yours are, we are enabled to do many things at the same time; an aspect of the self is able to accomplish one piece of work while another aspect, another. We are not limited. We have many 'bodies' at our disposal, not just one as you.

The questioner found this reply 'most thought provoking', wondering if even in our 'boxed-in' incarnate state, where we identify solely with our conscious selves, we are able (and not only during sleep) to do more than one thing at a time without intrusion upon the privacy or simultaneous activities of the ego-self. She gave examples from some of her patients who reported experiencing her presence at moments of stress. 'At first I thought these presences might just be parts of their own larger selves given my form to symbolise their healing aspect. This could be true but it could also perhaps have been one of my "thousand selves" answering a call for help.' She asked me to read her letter to Nabraham, requesting particularly his reaction to this final paragraph:

Q. These are encouraging thoughts to bear in mind when as little selves we feel singularly helpless, either because we have no power to change some unhappy situation in society, or because we are too old or crippled or ill to do all we would like to for others or for the world. Perhaps at other levels we are more busy than we know, answering calls, spreading ideas, doing with other less hampered levels of ourselves some of the things we would so like to do 'down here' but cannot. If we are all so many selves, what power we have to improve things. And how important it is to realise that our larger self exists and give it the positive support of thinking constructively and not being negative and despondent because consciously we seem so helpless.

Nabraham (through Jessica). The lady has indeed got the message, and we are so greatly pleased that we have been able to get it through, for the difficulty of giving *meaning* to our words is the hardest task. Words come readily but the meaning can so easily be misinterpreted. That is why we may have to repeat the same thing in different ways. Sometimes we have to provoke your imagination to convey meaning since words are often inadequate.

As the lady says, it is indeed true that those who are developed enough, even in the incarnate state, can be of service in different ways and in doing several things at the same time. Very often, when the physical body is incapacitated, the soul is more easily enabled to attend to many matters simultaneously. This is what is meant by the term 'acting without acting' or 'doing without doing'.

The powers of thought and feeling are to be known more and more in the times to come. Directed and attuned thought *is* the greatest power, and it is this idea which we wish to impart to the people. If it were more widely known and realised, we would more quickly reach the peace and conditions on earth which are so desirable.

We trust that you can imagine the soul, who is free of all limitations, accomplishing apart from the body many tasks and answering many calls at the same time, for the soul is out of time and space, above and beyond all duality.

THE NATURE OF SOUL

The first exercise in general teaching, attempted by Louisa in 1983, was in response to a friend who had already received personal messages from Nabraham. This friend, who worked with clergy, questioned the soul's attitude to abortion.[8]

Nabraham. Soul is essentially a matter of conditions — it is a becoming — a principle of degree: it can grow, it can diminish. Soul is the spirit of love. It is not to be found in all persons. The soul can retract from the body when con-

---

8. Subsequently printed in *New Humanity*, Oct/Nov 1988, No. 83.

ditions are not suitable. The soul hovers nearby and waits, hoping that the person will become able to receive the soul again. Soul intermingles with the mind and body; it is like another body but is an essence which pervades thought and action. Soul is an informing principle for the spirit, which links us to all other beings.

We begin simply as a sentient being in the womb; we do not think; we are aware of our feelings or somatics; we are receivers.

We are born, and the brain begins to process information; it begins to participate actively in the world.

At around five to ten weeks we may smile. This is the first instance of the soul entering the child. 'Entering' is not the right word; it is a pervading, mingling, or co-existing with. Soul is an essence with no beginning and no end; there are not moments of soul being, but degrees of soul being. A small child is very close to soul and can see and understand soul more fully than do adults. Soul dims with experience of learning and the vicissitudes of life. It does no good to seek so actively for a time of soul entering. Soul is with the child as it grows in the womb. Soul hovers beside the mother and informs her with a loving principle.

There are, however, some conceptions which are not welcome, and soul is total love and does not impose itself upon a mother who does not welcome the child. It leaves her to her own decisions. Soul would never enforce itself upon any being. Soul has only the principle of love; it is not loving to stay close to the psychic space of one who is in misery at the child's conception and who does not welcome soul. Soul has many opportunities for life attachment. It matters little to soul if one opportunity is not suitable; others will come. Soul is utterly patient and understanding. Termination of a pregnancy does no harm; as with spontaneous miscarriage it is often the kindest solution to an unwanted pregnancy. Soul seeks only kindness and loving acceptance by the mother; also it seeks only these things for the mother. Soul is total love.

118

You have discovered the way to save infants; when once many died very young, many pregnancies were needed to secure just a few lives. This is not so for you now, and termination is a sensible and kind answer to unwanted pregnancy. Contraception is even more sensible; it restores the natural balance of survivors which you have altered with advanced medical care. You do not live in the dark ages when infant mortality was more common than survival. Soul reigns only in the conditions of love and acceptance; it is cruel and unkind to force a woman to care for an unwanted child whose struggles — although enlightening in the final perspective — are not compatible with the principle of soul. There always will be opportunities for each soul to experience whatever is needed for growth. There is a group of Brothers who take care and plan for the needs of soul.

It serves no purpose to soul that the mother should suffer in any way by continuing an unwanted pregnancy. If you can see that soul is not an immediate or impatient essence, then you can see that the suffering of the mother is alien to the principle of soul. The mother will certainly experience whatever her life purpose is whether or not the child is carried and born. Follow only those principles of love and kindness to the mother, and soul will grow in the world, not just stand beside us waiting for these conditions. Soul is eternal and there is no need to be anxious for one opportunity to incarnate. The mother herself needs understanding, love, kindness, acceptance; she will know which course of action to follow. Within herself will be the answers to the problem. She will find these answers with the help of those who only wish love and kindness for her. Guilt and shame play no part in soul's actions; those who would, by their rigid views and doctrines, make such a woman suffer so are themselves far removed from soul. A mother herself will know if it is unkind to bear a child for whom she shall have no love or sympathy. A mother will know if she can grow with the pregnancy into love for the child. Only help such

119

mothers to find the solution within by standing beside them in support and understanding for one who seeks to find the answers within.

Cot deaths occur where the soul recognises that the life purpose is just to be for a little while in this world.

You have much to unlearn in the ways of the spirit which is love — and only love.

Understandably, readers of our original records differed more sharply in reaction to this subject than to any other, some finding it wise and pertinent, others taking exception.

One friend of considerable standing in the psychic and healing fields, with a background of esoteric knowledge both theoretical and practical, approved the script 'as far as it went' but considered it inadequate since so many important aspects were omitted. In particular he instanced the viewpoint of the incarnating (or reincarnating) soul who had undertaken to descend through progressively denser levels in order to take on the physical state only to be rejected. While agreeing that the script could indeed have been more comprehensive, we explained that it was written specifically for those in church circles who might be put off by concepts involving pre-existence, let alone reincarnation. Selective presentation is crucial. However, further elucidation was forthcoming.

Nabraham. To understand this issue we must first understand the essential difference between soul and personality. Here in your world you 'feel' things like rejection at the personal level, and so you imagine that a soul prevented from a specific incarnation also feels such rejection. This is not so. The soul has no dealings with such negative reactions, indeed it is incapable of feeling such things. It is completely above the trivia of personality. We can only reiterate, as in the original abortion text, that soul is complete love and acceptance, complete patience and total understanding; it wishes only for the good and happiness of other beings. The path it follows is harmlessness and benevolence. It cannot suffer defeat or rejection for it is not within its capacity to 'feel' such things which are of the personality,

120

the 'small self'. Can you separate body, mind and personality from the soul essence? When you ask such questions it is because you operate from the small self's belief that an individual has certain rights of existence or being. This is not so for soul, which exists beyond the physical or psychic realms. Soul cannot experience rejection for it does not have that small-self sense of personal rights. It operates purely from a position of otherness or of non-self.

The bias of your question is upon the assumption that soul denied incarnation will react as a personality denied something to which it has a right. You must make a quantum leap beyond this assumption of personal rights if you are to grasp the essence of soul which suffers only by the sufferings of others. Soul is that essence which Jesus spoke of as the Father who forgives, accepts, understands and knows all human weakness. The soul abhors the pain and suffering of mankind and so will do nothing, nothing, which can cause such suffering. Even by incarnating to a woman who has no ability to welcome the child, soul would rather lovingly retreat than cause her harm. Such is the love of soul that it prefers to step aside than cause suffering. The struggle you speak of for the waiting soul does not exist; the passing between the worlds by soul is as easy as the flight of a feather upon a gentle wind. Death is such a passing; the body and mind may struggle but those who have witnessed death know that, once the struggles are given up, the person is filled with the radiance of soul which passes in serenity, joy and glory, bestowing upon those who witness it a sense of awe and wonder. If you can catch the essence of spirit for a brief moment you will understand that such questions are without foundation, like asking the sun if it suffers when the clouds prevent its rays from shining upon the earth. The sun shines on regardless, and the soul flourishes on in love regardless of man's actions.

Whether the original draft was not clear or was not read with sufficient care, several readers queried the apparent assumption that some people completely lack a soul, the alarming sentence being, 'It is not to be found in all persons'. One wrote, 'I have met this idea before of not everyone having a soul. It is quite different from being materialistic and unaware of its existence.' Another, although valuing the description of what she termed 'the substance of soul' declared, 'On the other hand I am appalled at the idea that not everyone has one. Or does it mean temporarily lost?' Clarification was obviously necessary.

Nabraham. As to the specific 'soulless' individuals, we understand your horror at such an idea, but what you must see is that each individual is reared in such a way that either encourages or discourages soul contact. Soul is always present, but not always informing the person's thinking. It is *contact* with the soul which is lost, not the soul itself. There are no soulless persons, only degrees of soul contact.

Clearly he felt that for our truer perspective the subject should be set in a wider frame, so he launched into an historical and sociological world overview.[9] First, a definition:

Nabraham. The nature of soul is benevolence, compassion, and respect for all God's creation. This concept encapsulates the original nature of mankind.

There are those who believe that humanity is basically bad and must be taught to live socially by cultural taboos and laws. However, we would like to affirm that this is not so. The basic nature of people is good, and culture can be the tool which turns it from this natural state. Primitive humans lived at ease with their fellows, much as the gorilla in family groups, and all in that group had a place. All received affection and consideration accordingly. Bands and members very rarely acted in violent ways which could cause real harm to others. Leadership was by demonstration and symbolic ritual. Thus human nature was influenced by

---

9. Selections were printed under the title of 'Establishing Soul Rule' in *New Humanity*, August/September 1988, No. 82.

the soul which furthers the whole group and only does those deeds which bring success to its members.

Unfortunately mankind has lost touch with this primitive ease and must now contend with extremes of overcrowding which stretch the natural abilities for benevolence. We have left the garden of Eden where there was enough space and time for soul to flourish. We are governed no less now by survival instincts than when we were nearer to the animal kingdom in brain capacity. Severe overcrowding creates stress and mental illness whereby our natural benevolence — the soul's influence — is pushed to its limits. We have learned to eliminate much natural wastage of damaged and maladjusted bodies, so there are now too many individuals who must get along with too little space and resources for natural comfort, i.e. the comfort of emotional and physiological needs. This has created the need for stronger and stronger social constraints and laws; these work to a certain degree to control behaviour but can never replace the influence of soul from within.

Rogues in the primitive wilderness were turned away from the group to mend their ways or live alone whereby they could do no damage to the group. In modern civilised worlds these rogues often become the entrepreneurs and extremists who thrive and damage the group. Many of the problems you now face are due to these types of individuals who grasp power, commodities and status to gain great personal wealth at the expense of the group. What is necessary for the original natural order to be restored is intelligent, large-scale, group-oriented thinking rather than individualistic gain at the price of others. Men and women can organise their world so that all are able to thrive and flourish without the need for violence and competition which rob the planet of its dignity and cause neighbouring groups to fight.

World government and ordering of resources on an international scale would resolve the conflicts and stresses which modern people face daily, and create a world where soul can flourish again. A vast operation is needed led by people who think in terms of planetary wholeness — the next soul level to group soul thinking — a shift of consciousness to establish soul rule and create a new atmosphere where enemies simply do not exist. Individuals with such soul values could turn nations from enmity to cooperation.

Culture and family background have a great influence on the degree of soul contact an individual may reach. Culture changes with survival needs and the pressures of over-crowding and poverty. Loving, caring and compassionate rearing ensures soul contact; harsh or undisciplined rearing can hinder it. Thus there are degrees of soul contact which an individual attains. No personal blame is involved for it is a matter of conditions rather than of personal initiative in the beginning stages. But, once upon the Path, individuals may redeem soul's teachings by initiative and diligence. Some cultures and groups, by remaining true to their beliefs and protected by their rituals, have maintained soul contact even within a heavily populated and materialistic society.

Even so, most of the world is indeed in a sadly soulless state today; many are insanely out of touch with soul, emotionally bereft and crippled by this divorce. Some never get the chance to learn of soul before its influence is knocked out of them by rough handling and harsh conditions. However, none is ever lost, for soul does not leave the person; it stands patiently by for the opportunity to re-establish contact and re-educate. There are very very few individuals who knowingly turn away from soul's path, as in the Faust myth. Most turning away is due to ignorance and the unnatural way humans are now forced to live. Moreover, those who do not know soul will not necessarily be evil or do bad things, for culture and law often keep them in line with society and they appear to be essentially pleasant people. Do not fear for those who do not know their soul, for those who do know wield the greater influence which shall order the world in the final reckoning. Your world will be restored to its natural order and balance. As you grow and learn you will bring with you the next phase of the evolution of soul.

Received in April 1988, this was the last message Louisa brought through for this book, apart from the Appendix. As is shown in the Evaluation, she was becoming progressively more aware of the theme — the concept — which Nabraham was endeavouring to transmit, rather than (as formerly) each word as it came. At the end, therefore, she wrote:

The idea behind this message is that the world at present is in a transitional stage between two states of relationship to soul: the original naïve state of primitive people and the enlightened state of self-conscious humanity. Between the two is a kind of no-man's-land where mankind can lose touch with soul. This happens in a micro- and macrocosmic ontology, i.e. to the individual and to humanity as a whole across developing ages. Thus the child and early mankind had a natural access which can be obscured by growth and change. The second phase of soul contact is a greater, broader awareness at both instinctive and rational levels: heart and head, emotion and intellect, united in harmony.

It may be of interest that this script was given before the first showing of the second part of the TV documentary on Easter Island (Horizon, BBC2, 18.4.88). The programme clearly illustrated the transition from the first stage to the 'no-man's-land', describing the loss of contact with soul as shown by the destruction of the great god-statues. This came as a result of overcrowding, consequent deforestation and soil erosion, followed by warfare — a microcosm of what is now happening on the whole planet.

Individually, too, it appears that the whole matter, at the level of pre-incarnational choice, is far from simple. In Louisa's absence, Jessica received the following qualification in reply to a question about the re-education after death of those who had lost soul contact.

Nabraham. There are souls within the group family who do take on the limitation of loss of contact with the family soul for the express purpose of some part of the plan for which they are, as you might say, instruments; for in order to bring about some express task it is needful that they appear ignorant. It is only after your so-called death that the task can be seen in its fullness and recognition of the necessary condition of ignorance be made.

So, there is indeed a great mystery.

CHAPTER SIX

AN EVALUATION

A Critique of Channelling — Afterword — Comment from a Discarnate Guide — Conclusion

A CRITIQUE OF CHANNELLING[10]

In early 1987 a good deal of both critical and creative discussion occurred on 'channelling' which was expanding rapidly in many forms and at different levels particularly in America. The subject arose in network meetings, lectures, private letters, and was mentioned in relevant journals. Also in question were the validity of the psychic function and the assumption, use and abuse of 'guides' and 'masters'.

Such challenges are healthy. At this point in the training experience, therefore, it seemed to me appropriate for us all to study the literature and differing views, to ask Nabraham for his opinion, and to engage in some self-assessment.

JESSICA'S CONTRIBUTION

Traps and the astral level

The description of 'a morass of hidden dangers and traps' I totally agree with. I am very aware of this myself, feeling

---

10. Subsequently published in *Light*, Spring 1988.

conscious of the responsibility towards the *effects* of 'channelling'. Maybe this is why I have so much self-distrust and self-criticism when I answer questions. People who are gullible and looking for guidance, trying to find their own paths, will be taking in and allowing themselves to be influenced by my answers. What if I'm wrong?

I do agree that there is too much of the (worst) 'spiritualist church' type of medium speaking on platforms to lost, gullible people, thus giving the valid teachers and the White Brotherhood less chance and less credibility when they show up through channels such as Ruth and others. I also see that this art can be misused in duping and extracting money out of the credulous. The blind acceptance by these credulous people too bothers me greatly. I certainly wouldn't want followers and pupils gathering round me, hanging on to my every word. I would much sooner show them how to find their own inner sources than that they should rely on mine.

I agree that the astral levels have to be cut through, but as to whether they are a necessary step on the way in experiencing all levels, I'm not sure. Maybe as the yoga teachings all say, it is the astral level itself which is the trap that many fall into, remaining stuck there instead of pushing on and through it. I have a feeling that this is where many of the channellings are coming from, and it is this level which produces the glamour, making it all the more difficult to leave behind. I remember this well myself during the time when I first began contacting past lives and writing messages. Feeling myself to be gifted, it was difficult to throw off that glamorous sensation of being special. Even now I am having to make great efforts with myself regarding my clients. It would be so easy, so very easy, to give messages and guidance through Nabraham, but in every case I have worked towards getting them in touch with their own source. It has been a temptation that I have been well aware of. I can quite see how easy it is to fall into that trap of allowing clients to depend on me and my guidance for their

128

way out of their problems instead of learning to be independent. I am all too aware of the way people in my position could easily take advantage of this gift, talent or whatever, and do so unscrupulously.

I also agree that one doesn't need to be psychic in order to receive inspiration. In fact I would hazard a guess that the people who are not psychic would have greater purity and less interference from the glamour of the astral, psychic level.

The problem of publishing teachings

It had been suggested that if teachings were issued under the name of a recognised guide, they might be more acceptable as having greater authority than if written directly from the 'channel'; on the other hand they might equally be rejected unread by sceptics of mediumship. Should the sensitives take full responsibility (even if acknowledging the origin as from their higher selves) instead of sheltering behind a named communicator?

I have not found the answer to this myself yet, so cannot comment. To ask Nabraham *could* be an opting out of responsibility in certain cases, but in one instance of a close family relationship I knew that if I answered from my ego I should over-react, so I asked whether the person would accept a message from Nabraham, which she did. It was wise and objective, putting the issue in a wider context than I could have seen. It all depends on circumstances and on the nature of the recipient.

Blending: duality and unity

The idea had been suggested that relationship with inner sources could perhaps be understood on a physiological level in terms of conversations between the right and left hemispheres of the brain. In our Western, rational, left-brain culture, we may often be relatively unconscious of the intuitive, creative wellspring of the

129

right brain. Therefore, to become whole we need to recognise and blend with it, finally achieving a balance of both sides, when communication becomes communion.

I can quite honestly say that in my own experience I know that in the beginning when you (Mary) used to write down what I was saying I could remember nothing until you read it back to me. But as I gradually learned to write the messages myself, I found that I was beginning to know and remember more and more as I was writing it. And now I find I am aware of what I am writing most of the time, although obviously I cannot remember word for word until I read it back as I am too busy concentrating on what is coming through at the time. But without reading it through straight away I am able to say what the message was in words of my own. I can give the gist of it, so I am increasingly aware of what is being communicated.

I totally agree with 'communication' becoming 'communion' and then merging into union. I feel this to be the goal of communication and something for which I am striving myself. I cannot explain how I know, but the simplest way I can put it is to say that I am aware of duality, and in union there is the oneness, not twoness. In communication there is always 'the other' whereas in communion all is One.

My feeling is that while we still exist in the realm of duality, a teacher, guide or guardian angel is necessary, and hence the stage of development which requires our leaning on and learning from this other, whether it be an outer guru or teacher or an inner guru or teacher. But I cannot see how the goal of Union, Self-realisation, God-realisation, can be achieved while we rely on this other. For the other itself implies duality, and in union there is no sense of other — all *is* One. As Jesus said (perhaps when he himself reached this point), 'I and my Father are one,' meaning that duality no longer existed for him and henceforth he existed in his own right, in his own name, without needing to refer to his guardian angel or his Father saying this, that and the other.

130

In fact, he no longer had the identity (to himself) of Jesus; he *was* the Father and the Father doeth all.

Shortly after writing this essay, Jessica asked Nabraham for his views on the current controversies. He took a more inclusive line.

Nabraham (through Jessica). In commenting on the viewpoints, we would only like to say that the note sounded is always the key to the authenticity of intercourse with the Elder Brethren. The names which we are given matter little, and it is good to remember that we are, as we say, Elder Brethren and therefore teachers of our brethren on earth who aspire to the spiritual realms of light and truth. Whatever is given out which will reach humanity as a whole needs only to be considered by its quality, and not by any high-sounding name or authority, for very few as yet are in any way near contact with those great ones whose time and energy are spent almost entirely on larger matters.

We ask that you spend little time in criticism and even less in listening to it, for much energy is lost in this way. Whatever is given out which gives food for thought and is based on love and adoration, respect and gratitude, and raises the awareness of all, then this is good. True inspiration leads to that perfect trust and peace within, which no criticism can ever remove or cause to waver.

Accept that those who cling to emotional and mental levels and cannot venture beyond them will always doubt and criticise that which they do not know, until their own experience teaches them. By quietly and faithfully doing one's best to keep inner contact with the light of one's soul or higher self, one's radiation and influence will be increasingly felt. It is this radiation and influence that will tell much, and the speech less, so look to the radiation of those whose viewpoint interests you.

Since this is Louisa's story, I asked her for a self-assessment.

LOUISA'S CONTRIBUTION

How do I begin to assess my relationship to Nabraham and the Brethren? I can only assess it subjectively and tell how it has beautified and intensified the way I experience living. In other words I can only tell how I feel about my life. The relationship is intensely personal and yet it reaches out beyond the little me.

I remain essentially unchanged by it and yet everything about me and my life is better for it: more beautiful, wondrous, exciting, more real. I am still the same me: an earthy type, serious and introverted at times and yet socially at ease; the extraverted introvert, I laugh easily, enjoy myself immensely and also cry desperately. I am ultrasensitive to how other people feel which can be painful; I am a grumpy bear in the mornings and a pussycat after lunch; I am obsessively equalitarian and shamefully self-indulgent; I suffer a little from guilt and a lot from arrogance. In short I have my share of human failings and strengths. I do like myself very much, both good and bad. Nabraham taught me this and I am eternally grateful. Self-acceptance and self-love lead to acceptance and love for others; as Nabraham often says, 'love ever becomes' in my life. I love living; mostly my days are a joy and a gift. I love serving the Brethren and revere their loving friendship, benevolent wisdom and joyful humour. I have learned so much and have much more to learn.

As a psychologist and a Sun/Capricorn I am essentially a realist and do not take easily to flights of fancy. I am comfortable with my feet on the ground and with facts rather than fantasy. I try to keep a fluid approach neither closing doors too close nor welcoming new worlds too readily. I am super-critical, both of myself and others; critical not in the negative, punitive sense but in the empirical sense of seeking validity. I still cannot definitely say that Nabraham exists in the objective 'out there' reality. It is possible that he is a substratum of my own personality, an

132

unconscious part of myself. I cannot state absolutely that I believe in life after death, discarnate beings, or spiritual worlds. I can only state that these things are possible and use these concepts to help in the here and now struggle. Essentially it is the quality and benevolence of the communications which I can absolutely value rather than their source. I can remain open to doctrines, beliefs and value systems; basically they all revolve around the key concept of love. And love is whatever you perceive and learn it to be. The essence of Nabraham's advice and teachings is love, the kind of love which loves all other loves.

Working with and knowing Nabraham is an integral part of my life; it enhances and enlarges the quality and depth of my life through love. I am utterly grateful to him, as I am to Mary and Jess who help me know and live more in this spirit of love and kindness to every living thing.

Mediumship is a path which requires discipline and dedication to self-development. It should not be taken lightly; it is a gift with heavy responsibilities. Even so, the rewards are great and the pleasure enduring. Anyone who would also travel this path should know that it takes many years, many tears, and courage to refine oneself. Brutal self-honesty and an unquenchable sense of humour also seem to help. Whatever else I have learned it is this: pain passes, love endures. Both are essential to the path.

It has not been easy to follow, there has been much suffering. But it has been worth it. I cannot measure its worth in words. I can only try to help others find their paths; this is how I can best express its worth.

AFTERWORD FROM MARY[11]

As stated in the introduction, I have not the qualifications to set out to train mediums. However, having worked alongside

---

11. Subsequently published in *Light*, Summer 1988.

Louisa, Jessica and several other developing sensitives for some 25 years, now is the time to ask what I have learned. This contribution comes purely from my own findings.

Respect

I have learned, once committed, to trust the process; to move with the natural rhythm of growth even though preparation may last for half a lifetime; never to try to force or hurry development. This attitude involves recognition of, and respect for, some of the early and possibly crude manifestations which may often be the only ways in which the 'other side' can at first break through. Thus, some sensitives I have known begin by experiencing flashes of light, strange sounds, even minor poltergeist phenomena, or they may discover their ability as an unconscious agent for movement of glass or ouija board. Others experience the sixth sense first through those dreams which seem as real as daily life if not more so; or through imaging, meditation and visions they see their teacher's face and form, perhaps hearing his words spoken in their minds. (It is important that such initial experiences should not be automatically rejected as 'only my imagination'; imagination is a most valuable faculty which needs to be respected as the way through to other levels of reality.) Again others may be unable to hear, see, or even imagine anything, yet are aware of intuitive hunches, meaningful happenings such as being drawn to a certain book, and even to those pages relevant to their present needs, and other apparent coincidences which outweigh the laws of chance.

Education

Here I can speak with more authority, having worked in this field all my life. In the word's true meaning of 'leading forth that which is within', it is vital to encourage the development of psychic and spiritual faculties to as high and pure a level as possible. During the early part of this process I cannot over-emphasise the value of some form of psychological self-work so that a sound balance of personality may be achieved before venturing into relatively uncharted areas of consciousness. (But here, as a psychotherapist, I recognise that I am probably prejudiced and that this is not everyone's way.) It does, however, prevent people with strong but uncontrolled psychic powers going over the edge into neurosis or at worst psychosis. Sometimes the lower levels have to be worked through (see pp. 83–91) but usually harmlessly if the psyche is sound and thoroughly oriented to the light.

Orientation to the highest one can reach at each stage is of supreme importance. The form or idiom must be congenial to the individual, for example in the choice of a church, brotherhood group, or training course inspired by the Ageless Wisdom. In such a community — or even in pairs or alone — the sensitive may find various forms of ritual helpful, not only in orientation but also for essential protection especially during vulnerable times of crisis and change. Here the need for trust, discipline and plenty of practice comes in.

As time goes on, the sensitive becomes increasingly aware of the different levels of communication contacted, recognising inner teachers by the varying quality of their vibration (or spiritual fragrance as one termed it). Thus a 'helper' is registered on a frequency different from that of the usual teaching guide (see p. 68); on rare occasions the atmosphere is heightened for all present when a Great Teacher or some higher being comes through (see p. 77).

Personal dedication to the work occurs consciously at the appropriate time for each individual but must, of course, be freely willed as it can well be a life commitment. Frequently it needs reiteration at crucial intervals. Sometimes dedication is recognised as having already been made, perhaps before birth by the higher self, yet even so the present personal ego must say 'Yes'.

As part of the educational process, and forming a natural follow-through from preliminary psychological work on relationships, some form of outer service is almost inevitable. It may take any form such as one of the creative arts or crafts, scientific research, teaching, healing or counselling, according to the abilities and interests of the individual. Like the parable of the talents, the sensitive's own development requires this outer contribution so as to provide for a healthy flow of the new energies; instead of becoming congested and possibly stagnant, their inflow increases in proportion to the outflow. However, at the initial stage of over-enthusiasm it is vital not to become exhausted and drained (though most of us have to learn through this experience). Spiritual power comes *through* and not *from* the personality, and each sensitive needs to find and keep the right point of balance — not easy.

In this book we have been concerned specifically with those sensitives learning to cooperate with the inner Teaching Brotherhoods, giving service in that special field.

In practising transmission of teachings it is wise from the outset to distinguish clearly between two processes: the creative and the critical. When they are confused, many students I know experience a lack of confidence to the extent that the flow of communication is distorted, crippled or even completely stifled. I have found that, especially in the initial stages, two separate mental processes are involved: the inspiration bubbling up through the creative well-spring of the right hemisphere of the brain; and the conscious, logical left-brain activity which assesses and discriminates. Both are necessary but at least in the practising period should not occur at the same time, and here discipline comes in. After due orientation and protection, the sensitive should 'hand over', allowing the unknown to emerge whether orally, in automatic writing, dictation through normal script, or telepathically in ideas and images. Not until afterwards comes the critical assessment. Some of the material is bound to be influenced by the human mind

136

and feelings, indeed the teachers recognise and make use of this (see pp. 139–40). We need to accept not only that each sensitive's special abilities and qualities will be seen as necessary instruments but that some strongly held personal views may well slant the message. Continual practice will give an increasing proportion of validity, a greater acceptance of some inevitable fallibility, and awareness of those possibly dangerous areas of emotional involvement which should be wisely avoided until cleared. Confidence increases as the balance between the creative and critical aspects is established. I have not worked in depth with those who err on the side of indiscriminate and uncontrolled 'inspiration' probably because they tend to lose incentive when faced with essential disciplines, but I have met them. In their case, in the first high flush and glamour of discovery, more weight should be given to discernment and judgement.

Phases in conscious development

Here I am writing from only limited experience, but from the material it would seem that the more mature the personality, the greater is the increase of awareness and unity between communicator and sensitive. Although no firm boundaries can be drawn, I have found approximately three stages:

(a) The phenomena are experienced as 'wholly other' from the conscious ego identity. I have never worked with anyone in trance, although I have had extensive experience of being at the receiving end. But in the early stages of preparation, when engaged in past-life work and inner journeys, Jessica used to put herself into an altered state of consciousness. She explains (see p. 130) that when Nabraham first appeared in these journeys she was completely unaware of what she had relayed to me until it was read back to her on regaining normal consciousness. Parallel states of dichotomy would be those experiences from 'outside' such as phenomena of lights, sounds and movement of objects. Also in this category are those 'real' dreams so totally different from waking life. Automatic writing can come at first with no conscious participation by the sensitive other than willingness to hold the pen. At this stage the content of the communication can appear 'evidential' in so far as it is foreign or even opposite to the sensitive's own *conscious* ideas or previous knowledge.

(b) As the personality is cleared and spiritual awareness increased, it is found that the higher the level, the more the so-called objective and subjective experiences approach one another. The sense of the words is remembered and felt at the time; images, ideas and telepathy supersede mere verbal communication; indeed the true depth of meaning may well be sensed as existing beyond the sensitive's ability to grasp, so that still further growth is needed. As in the experience of inspired artists and musicians, the content of the teaching may emerge as a meaningful whole in a higher dimension, a total pattern which has to be brought through and spread out in our linear space/time by means of consecutive words and logical sequences. (The right and left hemispheres now appear to be participating in more conscious harmony, though it is hard work and sometimes beyond expression in our limited language.)

(c) A third stage, not often reached except in rare peak experiences, is that of blending where, as the mystics know, communication is deepened to communion. The sensitive just *is* and radiates (from a source beyond but now including the ego) wisdom and healing without words. I have shared with individuals and especially groups this timeless sense of unity with the higher worlds — an unforgettable experience.

The needs of our inner teachers

So far we have concentrated on training the mediums. We tend to forget the part played by sitters and questioners (whether present or through correspondence) for the inner teachers need us as much as we need them. In our experience they prefer not to pontificate; as true teachers they start from where their pupils are; they enjoy interchange in the form of questions and challenges; they need cooperation and feedback. Indeed at their own level they also learn and grow, as earthly teachers do, alongside their pupils. Our particular teaching group asked for carefully thought-out questions beforehand because it is our thoughts that they catch; they then prepare replies specifically geared to our capacity to understand. So it is a two-way process, a conversation, until as Jessica explains the twoness becomes oneness.

Paralleling this development in method it is found that the subject matter taught, received and discussed changes in level and quality from the personal, even occasionally trivial messages of early days to the exploration of increasingly unknown and abstruse areas of knowledge. In our case it will be noted that the development was in direct response to the quality of questions asked by the correspondents, in this way stretching the consciousness of all concerned.

COMMENT FROM A DISCARNATE GUIDE

Nabraham's contribution

We will try to give you our understanding of mediumship. It is like a path which an incarnate soul must discover among the many paths. It is not easy to find and not easy to follow. It leads to deeper awareness of self and others. The moral codes of the world cease to exist; as the disciple

139

follows the path he must find his own codes of conduct. These may change with time as the knowledge and trials of the path continue. The path brings with it many severe tests and much deep soul-searching. It is not only a test of the character and strength but of the inner vision which is a special talent that the disciple creates from his own being. This talent differs with every individual; mediumship is not a simple skill but a blending of the whole personality and experience of the soul, heart and mind. Truly it requires the dedication of the total being of the person. Thus it becomes not just a skill but a way of being all the time, for during communication the act of mediumship is a simple enough skill in that the medium must tune in to the other world and relay the information — a mechanical process once the pattern is established. However, the whole life and breath of the medium becomes an act of communication to every other being who inhabits the two worlds. Thus, to describe and assess mediumship is in fact to describe and assess the person's relationship to the cosmos within and without. To describe the skill of communication is simple enough: it requires the stilling of the mind and a reaching in and out to us. We wait patiently to speak and you are only required to find that still, small space within your own psyche where we wait for you.

However, this simple enough act requires the individual's whole life and dedication to continue and develop into a real life path. So everyone who does find the skill is different in their unique way of bringing what they know to their use of the skill. The mind's vocabulary and conceptual powers will alter the way the teachings are explained, for we work within the understanding and scope of the individual. So it is necessary for us to give what that individual is capable of receiving. Teachers have a basic concept which flows through all the words, and only one idea is central. Loving understanding and acceptance are the basis.

CONCLUSION

by Nabraham

We stand before the gates of your vision and wait. We sing a joyful melody so that your inner ear can tune to the beauty of our world. We wait and watch for that moment of unity and we long to call to you that *here* is where the answers lie. We cannot make your lives easy. We can only help to give them more meaning and greater poise. We stand beside you and long to know that you will turn to us in your sadness or in your joy. For we are only in your creation and we become only by your permission.

By this we mean that we cannot ever speak or show ourselves unless the person actively agrees to this. We never intrude or go over any other being's rightful wishes. Thus we must have not only cooperation but permission in order to speak and be with a person. 'Existing only by your creation' implies that you must create the right conditions for us to exist in, so you create your own inner worlds and your own attitude to the world. By this act, or rather by these ongoing processes of creation, we can exist because the conditions become adapted to our requirements. Like fish, we can only exist in water and you create the right pool for us. We are independent beings and as such exist by our own light. However, it is only by your creation and permission that we can exist in *your* world.

We serve you and we love you as you go before the altar of life; we wait to be with you in every moment. So find your inner teacher and you will find the answers; you will find love and acceptance, you will find a better relationship to yourself. We have no instructions for living, no moral codes, and no enlightened doctrines. However, we can show you how to live in a spirit which gives only good things to yourself and others. This is all we would ask of you: give us your time and we are pleased.

GLOSSARY

Of some terms as used specifically in this book

Anima/Animus
Jungian terms for the archetypal energies of the female and male principles in us all. In a man, the *anima* is often relatively unconscious so, by definition, remains largely as an aspect of the 'Shadow' until he can consciously develop and integrate his feminine qualities in balance. The same is true of a woman in relation to her male *animus* qualities.

Archetypes
Patterns formed of living energies deriving from the collective unconscious of mankind. They often manifest in dreams and visions, taking the form of universal symbols and images, but needing specific interpretation for each individual. To the degree that we are unaware, we can be driven by their power. If, however, they are met and confronted consciously, as in psychological self-discovery and inner journeys, we can learn to relate *to* them and use their energies creatively, becoming more fully conscious and whole. For further detail, see Edwin C. Steinbrecher, *The Inner Guide Meditation*, Aquarian Press, Thorsons, 1988.

Astral
(See *Subtle Bodies and Worlds*)

Chakras, Centres
Psychically receptive and active energy centres interpene-

142

trating and affecting the physical as well as the subtle bodies, the link with the physical being through the endocrine system. The main chakras are often named as the crown, brow, throat, heart, solar plexus, sacral, and base of the spine. In psychic and spiritual development these centres are activated, but great care should be taken that the pace is slow and harmonious, and if possible under wise direction. The term *chakra* derives from Indian philosophy; for a clear and concise study of the Tantric model of the chakras and the subtle bodies, see Mary Scott, *A Renaissance of the Spirit: A New Way to See Ourselves*, Quest Books, The Theosophical Publishing House, 1988, Chapter 7.

Ego
The present conscious personality; the 'I' as we ordinarily know it. (*Not* the theosophical use of the term.)

Ego-shadow or Shadow
A Jungian term denoting that part of ourselves we would rather not own, so do not admit into full consciousness. In psychotherapy we discover and integrate it at progressive depths. First come the personal aspects which are often repressed from early childhood conditioning. Then some people may confront those aspects which they can manage of the collective Shadow — attitudes and energies ignored or denied by the society and race into which they incarnate.

Etheric
(See *Subtle Bodies and Worlds*)

Karma
An Indian term. The usual definition as the law of cause and effect (As you sow, so shall you reap) is over-simplified, applying in this retributive fashion mainly to those souls who can only learn, or who learn best, in such a rather stark way. White Eagle, Gildas, Nabraham and other teachers have stressed that the law is modified by infinite compassion, and

for the purpose of this book, which concerns those 'on the path', karma is seen as mainly redemptive. The operation of the law is too complex for us to comprehend fully from our incarnate level. For example, some appear to receive 'undeserved' suffering or limitation, whereas others who seem to 'deserve' them remain unscathed. This apparent unfairness can be understood only in relation to factors such as the age and specific needs of the soul; also the purpose for which incarnation takes place, remembering that some brave souls volunteer (at the higher self level) to redeem certain elements at some cost to the incarnating personality. Comprehension is aided when we realise that karma functions beyond the individual, in family, group, nation, race, and world ranges, so that what we achieve for ourselves we achieve also for all humanity. Further, we need not think of karma only in terms of negative aspects to be redeemed; innate 'gifts' are often karmically earned, then incarnated genetically, as are special conditions into which we are born.

Self

Spelled with a capital S, the Self is a Jungian term denoting the whole being, conscious and unconscious. At first, largely unconscious to the little ego, the Self guides us through life. The energy of the archetype of the Self strives always towards the synthesis of opposites in order to regain that unity existing beyond the 'fall' into diversity, aiming to link conscious with unconscious, ego with shadow, anima with animus, old wise man/woman with innocent child. As we grow in insight we pass through several 'mystical marriages' of such opposites within us, indicated by a variety of archetypal images and symbols. Ultimately the Self may manifest in the symbol of the Divine Child of Alchemy, reminiscent of Christ's saying, 'Except ye be converted, and become as little children, ye shall not enter into the kingdom of heaven.'

144

Subtle Bodies and Worlds

According to esoteric teaching, the physical body is the most dense of seven interpenetrating bodies, or energy fields, formed of 'substance' vibrating at ever-increasing frequencies. Clairvoyants are able to see at least some of the subtle energy fields as an aura surrounding a person. Terms vary, but most are derived from theosophical and Indian teachings. Closest to the physical is the *etheric* counterpart (see pp. 113–14). The denser part of this, sometimes known as the 'vital body' or replica, energises the physical during life but dissolves soon after death. The *astral* body (see pp. 127–9) comprises our emotions and attitudes. Beyond, but still interpenetrating the others, are the lower and higher mental energy fields extending up to the spiritual levels at an increasing range of finer substance.

As we expand our awareness, learning while still incarnate — and certainly after death — to live also in these bodies, we become conscious of corresponding worlds or planes of existence which themselves interpenetrate our earth and one another. The *astral* world or plane, sometimes called the 'plane of illusion', is 'ideoplastic' in that it is responsive to, and mirrors, our expectations and emotional attitudes. Thus for some it may be the beautiful 'Summerland' described by spiritualists; for others a bleak 'Winterland' of externalised, negative, habitual actions and reactions. And in between lies an intermediate zone, not so different from ordinary life on earth. If, however, we can develop finer thought and feeling while yet incarnate, at death our more developed subtle bodies will naturally gravitate to the equivalent level where they feel at home. An excellent survey of these planes is given in Paul Beard's *Living On* (see the following Suggestions for Further Reading).

SUGGESTIONS FOR FURTHER READING

1. GENERAL

Paul Beard, *Survival of Death*, first published 1966, latest edition 1988.
Paul Beard, *Living On*, first published 1980, latest edition 1987.
Paul Beard, *Hidden Man*, 1986.

This trilogy is published by Pilgrim Books, Lower Tasburgh, Norwich NR15 1LT. A most thoroughly researched, critical yet readable survey of conditions after death as described through mediums. *Living On* is particularly recommended.

D.M.A. Leggett, *The Sacred Quest*, Pilgrim Books, 1987.

A scholarly, broadly-based, and clear study of basic questions concerning life and death. Deriving from the author's own search, Dr Leggett leads us from scientific materialism to a spiritual understanding of the purpose of incarnation.

Arthur J. Ellison, *The Reality of the Paranormal*, Harrap, 1988.

Hailed as a landmark, written by a scientist who has also spent a lifetime investigating the paranormal, Professor Ellison demonstrates that in order to understand the nature of this reality we need to change the perceptions of our minds. Valuable for intelligent sceptics.

Lawrence Le Shan, *Clairvoyant Reality*, Thorsons, 1982.

A widely read book exploring the nature of reality as seen

by the medium, the mystic and physicist, with particular reference to paranormal skills.

Inexpensive *College Papers*, obtainable from The College of Psychic Studies, 16 Queensberry Place, London SW7 2EB. £1.00 each plus 25p for post and packing.
Ronald Fraser, *Changing Consciousness*, Paper 3.

F.W.H. Myers, *Scripts on the Process of Communication*, Paper 4.
Rev. Charles Fryer, *Life Beyond Death*, Paper 10.

2. SPECIFIC

(a) Mediumship

Grace Cooke, *The New Mediumship*, The White Eagle Publishing Trust, Rake, Liss, Hampshire, GU33 7HY, 1987.
Advice on how to unfold psychic gifts wisely and use them for spiritual service.

Helen Macgregor and Margaret V. Underhill, *The Psychic Faculties and their Development*, revised edition 1974, The College of Psychic Studies.
A sound, practical booklet especially useful for beginners.

Ivy Northage, *Mediumship Made Simple*, Psychic Press Ltd., 1986.
Based on extensive experience by a medium engaged in training potential mediums at The College of Psychic Studies.

Ruth White, *A Question of Guidance*, The C.W. Daniel Co. Ltd., 1988.
Written by an experienced sensitive and psychological counsellor, this book explores sensitivity, discriminates between different levels and kinds of inner guidance, gives valuable practical exercises for development, and emphasises that the search for guidance must be accompanied by personal psychological self-knowledge.

Jon Klimo, *Channeling*, Aquarian Press, Thorsons, 1988.

Coming from America, this is a comprehensive resource book, both contemporary and historical, providing a definitive study of channelling in every aspect.

(b) Examples of Teachings given through Mediums

White Eagle: catalogue of his many books obtainable from The White Eagle Publishing Trust, Rake, Liss, Hampshire, GU33 7HY.

Ruth White and Mary Swainson, *Gildas Communicates*, 1986.
Ruth White and Mary Swainson, *The Healing Spectrum*, 1986.
Both published by The C.W. Daniel Co. Ltd.

Ed. Michael Dean, channelled through Tony Neate from his teacher H-A: *The Guide Book*, Gateway Books, 1986.
A 'primer' giving practical advice about present life on earth.

Ivy Northage, *Spiritual Realisation: Inner Values in Everyday Life*, communicated by her spiritual teacher, Chan, Pilgrim Books, 1988.

Edited and with an introduction by Paul Beard, transmitted through Marie Cherrie, *The Barbanell Report*, Pilgrim Books, 1987.
Shows the changing outlook of a well-known spiritualist after his death. Valuable for stimulating discussion.

Jane Roberts' *Seth Speaks* (New York: Bantam, 1974) and *The Seth Material* (New York: Bantam, 1976) are two recommended books of many written by Jane Roberts as channel for her discarnate teacher, Seth.

SOME USEFUL ADDRESSES NOT ALREADY MENTIONED IN THE TEXT

The Findhorn Foundation, The Park, Forres, IV36 0TZ, Scotland.

A community offering educational programmes, conferences and workshops on an international scale.

Le Plan (in Provence), Le Petit Canadeau, Le Plan du Castellet, 83330 Le Beausset, France.

Founded in 1983 by Lorna St Aubyn, Le Plan is seen as part of a network of spiritual centres around the world whose purpose is to help the healing of the earth and humanity. Information on the wide variety of seminars held here can be obtained by writing to Lorna St Aubyn, 10 Irene Road, London SW6 4AL.

The Northumbria Seekers (Secretary: Pamela West, Holpeth House, Corbridge, Northumberland NE45 5BA.)

An educational association concerned with the spiritual nature of humanity and the holistic world view. Lectures and workshops are held mainly in Newcastle-upon-Tyne, so this centre is especially useful for those in the north of England and southern Scotland who find it difficult to travel to London.

The American Association for Parapsychology.

Provides information and career courses on metaphysics, transpersonal psychology, parapsychology and other related fields. You can obtain a free guidebook by writing to: American Association for Parapsychology, Box 225-A, Canoga Park, California 91305, U.S.A.

MEDIUMSHIP AND THE CHRISTIAN CHURCHES

When this manuscript had already been prepared for publication, our editor asked that two important questions be submitted to Nabraham. As always, the sisters did not see each other's messages, neither did they read my views (pp. 50–1) until afterwards.

Q1 How can one reply to a Christian minister who might suggest that the path of a medium is unchristian, as the church would say it is the clergy only who may mediate between God and the individual?

Nabraham (through Louisa). We can only suggest that whoever shall question your right to pass on the teachings should look to the teachings themselves, and then they shall see that there is nothing in these words which in any way will mislead a person. For the right of communion given to ordained preachers is a man-made right[1] and is conferred by man upon man; this is so that you can more easily know whom you may look to in your religious questioning. However, this right of communion is universal and is given to every soul by the laws of life itself. For each man and woman shall seek their own paths; in the end you can only accept that the true Godhead is within each individual and therefore each must have access to that communion.

---

1. Louisa's mind wanted to write 'communication' but Nabraham insisted on the word 'communion'. However, on questioning it was made clear that he was not referring to the Christian rite of Holy Communion.

Nabraham (through Jessica). This is an old, old problem which forever needs answering anew, for those in authority have always maintained the power and seek to retain that power. True authority needs no quarrel, for it has no competition. We would only say to those who fear another's path to look within themselves and to ask on what authority they speak. For the Lord himself, when asked by one of his chosen ones, said that any may heal and preach in the name of love whether they followed him or not, much to the rebuking of his chosen one.[2]

To those of the cloth, answer thus: all works done in love and charity are works of God, and no book of words can give any soul love where love does not exist. The true law and the true authority rest on love and love alone. Look to your love, we say, and there is no quarrel. The path is a means to an end, not an end in itself.

Although the sisters transmitted the same basic themes, it is interesting to note how Nabraham and his group (for this was definitely a group teaching) made use of the complementary personality 'lenses' to convey different aspects. This difference is particularly evident in the answers to the second question and in Jessica's final paper. For although both have a good balance between the love of God and of one's neighbour, I feel that whereas Louisa responds mainly to the nature of God as shining through human relationship and the brotherhood of mankind, seeing religion largely in terms of its moral and social aspects, Jessica is naturally a mystic seeking God through her inner vision of spiritual truth in a direct and, on occasion, uncompromising fashion. But this is just my opinion. What do readers think?

Q2 How can one answer the charge that the path of a

---

2. For those interested, the reference may be found in Mark 9:38–40, and Luke 9:49–50. The 'one rebuked' is John, the 'beloved disciple'. But Jessica reported no conscious recollection of having read or heard this passage even at school.

medium can lead to spiritual anarchy, whereas the church holds a single, unifying approach?

Nabraham (through Louisa). We must look to the books of religion for our rule in life and, as you say, these shall give us our common paths upon the earth. It is just and right that mankind must agree upon the acceptability of social actions. We do uphold the books of law; wherever you may be you must accept a certain standard of behaviour in order that there may be any degree of harmonious life. However, problems exist because some books differ from others, and then you have your religious conflicts and wars as in the Middle East and Ireland. Nevertheless there are certain basic laws in all religious law books, and we certainly uphold all these basic foundations. You may search for some shreds of evidence to prove differently, but you will find that they follow one rule only, which is the foundation of all others. That rule is that you must lead your life in such a way that you cause no unnecessary harm to another soul. This may appear facile but it is the only real base of any spiritual work. There can be anarchy only where people differ in their opinions as to how they should conduct themselves. We suggest no such thing as anarchy, and we reinforce the underlying principles of Christianity. Unfortunately, over two thousand years mankind has learned to interpret the basic teachings of Christ individualistically; thus you now suffer a divided church and a much divided outlook upon the meaning of the words of Christ. We do not wish to uproot or divide mankind; we wish to simplify and unify. You may find this difficult to believe if you are learned in specific interpretations of Christ's message, but if you read deeply you will realise the basics of which we speak and teach.

Q (Mary). Could you please deal more fully with that part of the question concerning mediumship?

Nabraham. The problem with mediumship is that it is so

152

very variable that it is practically of no use as a guide to living.[3] What we suggest is that mediumship is looked upon not as a guide but as an expansion of the basics. Its aim is to give greater depth and meaning to life rather than to instruct in the conduct of life. We know that there are levels of communion which produce nothing of value either to the medium herself or to those who listen. However, these stages are only steps upon the way. All mediumship should be treated as an apprenticeship in self-knowledge which is ultimately knowledge of God and the spirit worlds. Therefore we would advise no one to live their lives by the mediumship of another, but first to live by the rules and conduct of their society. Mediumship must not acquire any power to influence those who are unsure or unworldly, for they must first know how to live in the world. Thereafter mediumship is primarily a subjective apprenticeship to knowledge of one's own soul, and then, at successively higher and deeper levels, it is knowledge of the brotherhood of mankind — of the oneness of humanity. That unity in God which you describe is found within, and not by the books of religion. Mediumship is one of the paths to this knowledge. There are many other ways also.

Mediumship, being the contact with spirits or souls from other planes of existence, is much like painting. Although there are certain objective criteria which will always show what and where contacts are made, yet one may see whatever one chooses. We can only suggest that everyone who attempts or begins to develop contact must have a group of friends who can criticise objectively the results of such communion. For it is only the quality of the messages and the underlying degree of purity and love that show the source. New mediums must accept that they cannot become

---

3. Louisa felt that Nabraham meant 'If you go to three or four mediums for advice you may well get different messages from each. What we are emphasising is contact with your *own* source.'

instantly great painters other than by learning the trade.

The apprenticeship to pure communion where there is no problem of division and no negating influence is long, and so we do not uphold mediumship for its own sake, rather we uphold the path which is a purifying process alongside many other paths which also achieve this purity and enlightenment. So anyone who would undertake mediumship critically must need others to learn from. There is no instant answer to these questions but rather a way of looking at the path.

Louisa said, 'They are trying to describe it as an analogy to painting. You wouldn't dream of saying all painters must acquire the same technique, the same brushwork, the same ability to mix exactly the same colours. You wouldn't expect all artists to have acquired their excellence in the same way. Mediumship is similar; one acquires understanding by living. It is easier to be a Christian where a book of rules tells everyone how to behave. Mediumship is beyond the rules; it is a personal process as with a painter. Nevertheless it doesn't supersede the basic rule of not causing harm.'

Nabraham (through Jessica). This question too is age old and we reply as always in the spirit of love and helpfulness.

Those who have truth in their hearts will find that all paths lead to one goal, and it is the goal that should be looked at not the path. To quarrel with another's path is to invite criticism of one's own. Those whose view is such that their path and theirs alone is right have much to learn in regard to God, for God *is* the law; God is love and God is above your view of right and wrong. Those who have experienced this truth within themselves no longer fear differences of path or creed, for the truth has set them free of all dogma, creed and self-righteousness.

The single, unifying approach of a church may suffice those simple souls who wish — in fact need — authority to guide them, for they do not think for themselves. But for those strong souls who have, through their experience, gone beyond the need for parents or for any form of authority to tell them what is right, that approach is stultifying to their further growth. Furthermore it will be found that their authority lies within, and as our Lord said, this is the only place to seek for God. If God is not found within, He cannot be found in any book of words on no matter whose authority.

In conclusion may we add with regard to the path of mediumship that the disciplines imposed on such a one are great, and the path is strewn with many thorns and periods of great loneliness. Only the stouthearted, the dedicated and committed souls take this path, for the hardships endured would break a weaker soul. It is for this reason that many choose the simple, unifying approach of a Christian church, for inwardly they know that they are not ready or able to endure the loneliness and often great sacrifices which are demanded on the other path. There is a hierarchy of souls; all have their own places, and all can find themselves in their right place. Conflict, confusion and quarrel are the signs that a soul is in the wrong place or on the wrong path for his or her further growth.

If we extend the theme of the individual way to include mystical experience through other religions also, then a fitting ending to this book may well be the following passage by Jessica.[4] It describes a 'true dream' or vision experienced between 9 and 11 p.m. one evening when Jessica had gone early to bed, very tired. After it, she woke refreshed and spent most of the rest of the night writing it down, as she felt she must. Subjectively, she took the vision as a warning in her own life, for she had tried the many paths and had recently come to a temporary point of balance, stillness and peace beyond them all. This occurred ten years before our present book was written, and naturally there have been further tests and

4. Published under the title of 'Ultimate Reality' in *New Humanity*, December 1979/January 1980, No. 30.

insights, steep climbs and restful plateaus of peace. But the inner visions have guided her throughout them all.

It was as though I were a bird and had an overall view of a drama going on below me. First of all I saw a young man sitting cross-legged, meditating. He was dressed in the clothes of a Buddhist monk. While I watched, he suddenly went into an ecstatic state of bliss, from which he jumped up and proclaimed, 'I have seen God, I must go and tell the world what this bliss is like.' He called it Nirvana. I then saw him set off on his journey across the world, convinced he would set the world free.

The story then took me to another part of the world, to a room with strange signs and symbols on the walls and floor. A man sat at an altar with candles and incense and all sorts of paraphernalia. He was intensely absorbed in a pile of volumes, and, as I watched him experimenting and mumbling certain words, he suddenly stopped and a look of sheer joy came over his face. After a few moments he grabbed up his books and slung them into the fire. He shouted for joy, and proclaimed, 'I will tell the world I have merged with that Cosmic Consciousness.'

Then I went across the world to a place where a yogi sat concentrating. He was practising Raja Yoga, mind control. He too broke through into an utmost state of bliss and cried, 'It is Samadhi; I must tell the whole world how to get there.'

The next scene was in a little church where a man knelt in prayer. As I watched him, a great emotion overcame him, and he wept and cried, 'The Kingdom of Heaven, the peace which passeth all understanding. I will begin a Christian mission and tell all of this blessed state.' Off he went.

Finally, my story took me to a beautiful country scene by a stream. There sat a mystic, deep in thought, trying to find words to express his feelings for the beauty, the splendour of nature all around him. Suddenly his eyes caught the reflection of himself in the stream; his body went very still, a peace spread over his face, tears came into his eyes. He was transfixed, hypnotised, and held for what seemed ages. His brow smoothed out, the tension left his face, and an untold bliss came upon him. He grabbed his pen and his pad and scribbled away trying to describe this beauty and this love, for which he could find no name.

At this point I could see all these men travelling their different paths to tell the world. From different points on the earth eventually they all landed at the same spot, and, on meeting, began excitedly to convert one another. All were enthusiastically trying to tell of their experience. Much to their amazement, none could find words to convey the experience itself (there being no words to describe it anyway). One kept trying to explain that Samadhi was *the* ultimate experience; another was saying, 'No, Cosmic Consciousness is the ultimate reality, your experience is just a step on the way to this.' The Christian was frantically calling out, 'The Kingdom of Heaven is within; when you find that, you will have found peace and all your sins will be forgiven through Christ.'

I could see all this going on below me like a drama on the stage; in fact that is what it was, the great drama of life taking place, and the whole earth was the stage. From this point, the voices started to fade away and the scene carried on like play in mime. The figures were all striving to make their points, to assert their truth as the ultimate truth, all trying to convince the rest that their own truth was the highest and that if only the others would give up *their* experience of truth and see it as a trip of the mind, then they too would experience the ultimate. Each one of them was saying the very same things, yet each was convinced that he and he alone was right.

The voices were completely gone now, so all I could see and feel were their expressions and their inner feelings. I realised that each one had had his first taste of God, and also that they had all fallen into the same trap, the snare that awaits all who experience the reality for the first time. It was the snare of spiritual pride, whose offspring is arrogance which kills humility.

As I continued to watch the silent drama, I was shown that this subtle veil of pride prevented each of them seeing that their experiences were one experience; that there is only one ultimate reality, and therefore only one experience of it. It showed me that words, names, labels so often hide the truth, and that, if just one of those men had been able to see beyond his own set of symbols, names and words, he would have caught and realised the truth of the others' experiences, recognising them as the very same truth as his own.

I, too, now realise that the greatest tribute and praise we can ever give to God, or truth, is silence; and that one who has realised the true reality will instantly recognise another who has realised it, no matter what name each gave to its source. They will see and feel behind and beyond all words and names.

INDEX

abortion, 118–9
animals, 105
anxiety, 41
archetypes, 25, 142
astral level, 127–8

Beard, Paul, 21, 38, 58

Centre for Transpersonal
    Psychology, 32
chakras, 20, 142–3
channelling, 127
Christian Churches
    mediumship and the, 150–8
Churches' Fellowship for
    Psychical and Spiritual
    Studies, 51
co-existent lifetimes, 36–7
College of Psychic Studies, 21, 61
complacency, 41
conscious development
    phases in, 137–8
Cooke, Grace, 18, 59
dependence, 41
duality, 129–30

education, 56–9, 134–7
ego, 143
    and Self, 39–43
ego inflation/deflation, 40–1
ego-shadow, see Shadow
etheric brain/body, 113–4

Gildas, 29–33, 43

Gildas Communicates, 31
Grant, Joan, 30
group souls, 99–108
guide, inner, 48–50
    communication with the, 53–6,
        78–82
    contacting the, 37–9
Guirdham, Dr Arthur, 29, 57

Healing Spectrum, The, 31, 43
Hyde, Lawrence, 18, 21

independence, 41
inner journeys, 47–8

Jung, Carl Gustav, 17, 22, 24, 35,
    48

karma, 20, 23, 91–9, 106, 143–4
Klimo, Jon, 47, 59

mediumship
    preparation for, 59–62
mental hospitals, 87–9

negative influences, 87–9
New Age, 35, 43

past lives, 36–7, 91–9
population
    reincarnation and, 95–9
psychic faculties
    education of, 56–9, 134–7
psychic levels, 83–91

psychotherapy
  levels in, 35–9

Question of Guidance, A, 32

reality, 52
reincarnation, 91–9
religions, 49–50, 156–8

Self, 144
  and ego, 39–43
sense levels, 53
Seven Inner Journeys, 30
Shadow, 28, 43–5, 143, 115
siddhis, 50, 58
soul
  nature of, 117–26

and personality, 120–1
  see also group soul
Spirit of Counsel, The, 18
Steinbrecher, Edwin C., 54
subtle bodies, 53, 145
Swedenborg, Emanuel, 83, 85

time, 107, 108–17
training for mediumship, 47,
  59–62, 66–70, 134–9

unity, 129–30

Van Dusen, Wilson, 48, 83, 85

White Eagle Lodge, 18–22
White, Ruth, 29–33

STAY IN TOUCH

On the following pages you will find listed, with their current prices, some of the books and tapes now available on related subjects. Your book dealer stocks most of these, and will stock new titles in the Llewellyn series as they become available. We urge your patronage.

However, to obtain our full catalog, to keep informed of new titles as they are released and to benefit from informative articles and helpful news, you are invited to write for our bi-monthly news magazine/catalog. A sample copy is free, and it will continue coming to you at no cost as long as you are an active mail customer. Or you may keep it coming for a full year with a donation of just $2.00 in the U.S. ($7.00 for Canada & Mexico, $20.00 overseas, first class mail). Many bookstores also have *The Llewellyn New Times* available to their customers. Ask for it.

Stay in touch! In *The Llewellyn New Times'* pages you will find news and reviews of new books, tapes and services, announcements of meetings and seminars, articles helpful to our readers, news of authors, advertising of products and services, special moneymaking opportunities, and much more.

The Llewellyn New Times
P.O. Box 64383-Dept. 771, St. Paul, MN 55164-0383, U.S.A.

TO ORDER BOOKS AND TAPES

If your book dealer does not have the books and tapes described on the following pages readily available, you may order them directly from the publisher by sending full price in U.S. funds, plus $2.00 for postage and handling for the first book and 50¢ for each additional book. There are no postage and handling charges for orders over $50. UPS Delivery: We ship UPS whenever possible. Delivery guaranteed. Provide your street address as UPS does not deliver to P.O. Boxes. UPS to Canada requires a $50 minimum order. Allow 4-6 weeks for delivery. Orders outside the U.S.A. and Canada: Airmail—add retail price of book; add $5 for each non-book item (tapes, etc.); add $1 per item for surface mail.

FOR GROUP STUDY AND PURCHASE

Because there is a great deal of interest in group discussion and study of the subject matter of this book, we feel that we should encourage the adoption and use of this particular book by such groups by offering a special "quantity" price to group leaders or "agents."

Our Special Quantity Price for a minimum order of five copies of *Psychic Sense* is $29.85 cash-with-order. This price includes postage and handling within the United States. Minnesota residents must add 6% sales tax. For additional quantities, please order in multiples of five. For Canadian and foreign orders, add postage and handling charges as above. Credit card (VISA, Master Card, American Express) orders are accepted. Charge card orders only may be phoned free ($15.00 minimum order) within the U.S.A. or Canada by dialing 1-800-THE-MOON. Customer service calls dial 1-612-291-1970. Mail orders to:

LLEWELLYN PUBLICATIONS
P.O. Box 64383-Dept. 771 / St. Paul, MN 55164-0383, U.S.A.

THE LLEWELLYN PRACTICAL GUIDE
TO THE DEVELOPMENT OF PSYCHIC POWERS
by Denning & Phillips

You may not realize it, but you already have the ability to exercise and develop ESP, astral vision, clairvoyance, divination, dowsing, prophecy, and communication with spirits.

Written by two of the most knowledgeable experts in the world of Magick today, this book is a complete course—teaching you, step-by-step, how to develop these powers that actually have been yours since birth. Using the techniques they teach, you will soon be able to move objects at a distance, see into the future, know the thoughts and feelings of others, find lost objects, locate water and even people using your own no-longer latent talents.

Psychic powers are as much a natural ability as any other talent. You'll learn to play with these new skills, work with groups of friends to accomplish things you never would have believed possible before reading this book. The text shows you how to make the equipment you can use, the exercises you can do—many of them anytime, anywhere—and how to use your abilities to change your life and the lives of those close to you. Many of the exercises are presented in forms that can be adapted as games for pleasure and fun, as well as development.

0-87542-191-1, 256 pgs., 5 1/4 x 8, illus., softcover **$7.95**

THE LLEWELLYN PRACTICAL GUIDE
TO PSYCHIC SELF-DEFENSE AND WELL-BEING
by Denning & Phillips

Psychic well-being and psychic self-defense are two sides of the same coin—just as are physical health and resistance to disease: each person (and every living thing) is surrounded by an electro-magnetic force field, or aura, that can provide the means to psychic self-defense and to dynamic well-being. This book explores the world of very real "psychic warfare" of which we are all victims.

FACT: Every person in our modern world is subjected to psychic stress and psychological bombardment—advertising promotions that play upon primitive emotions, political and religious appeals that work on feelings of insecurity and guilt, noise, threats of violence and war, news of crime and disaster, etc.

This book shows the nature of genuine psychic attacks—ranging from actual acts of black magic to bitter jealousy and hate—and the reality of psychic stress, the structure of the psyche and its interrelationship with the physical body. It shows how each person must develop his or her weakened aura into a powerful defense-shield—thereby gaining both physical protection and energetic well-being that can extend to protection from physical violence, accidents ... even ill-health.

Denning and Phillips give exact instructions for the fortification of the aura, specific techniques (for personal and group use) for protection, and the Rite of the First Kathisma using the Psalms to invoke Divine Blessing. Unique "puts-you-in-the-picture" drawings enhance these powerful techniques.

0-87542-190-3, 306 pgs., 5 1/4 x 8, illus., softcover **$7.95**

THE LLEWELLYN PRACTICAL GUIDE TO ASTRAL PROJECTION
by Denning & Phillips

Your consciousness can be sent forth, out-of-the-body, with full awareness and return with full memory. You can travel through time and space, converse with non-physical entities, obtain knowledge by non-material means, and experience higher dimensions.

Is there life after death? Are we forever shackled by time and space? The ability to go forth by means of the Astral Body, or Body of Light, gives the personal assurance of consciousness (and life) beyond the limitations of the physical body. No other answer to these ageless questions is as meaningful as experienced reality.

The reader is led through the essential stages for the inner growth and development that will culminate in fully conscious projection and return. Not only are the requisite practices set forth in step-by-step procedures, augmented with photographs and "puts-you-in-the-picture" visualization aids, but the vital reasons for undertaking them are clearly explained. Beyond this, the great benefits from the various practices themselves are demonstrated in renewed physical and emotional health, mental discipline, spiritual attainment, and the development of extra faculties.

Guidance is also given to the Astral World itself: what to expect, what can be done—including the ecstatic experience of Astral Sex between two people who project together into this higher world where true union is consummated free of the barriers of physical bodies.

0-87542-181-4, 272 pgs., 5 1/4 x 8, illus., softcover **$7.95**

THE LLEWELLYN PRACTICAL GUIDE TO CREATIVE VISUALIZATION
by Denning & Phillips

All things you will ever want must have their start in your mind. The average person uses very little of the full creative power that is his or hers potentially. It's like the power locked in the atom—it's all there, but you have to learn to release it and apply it constructively.

IF YOU CAN SEE IT ... in your Mind's Eye ... you will have it! It's true: you can have whatever you want. However, there are "laws" to mental creation that must be followed. The power of the mind is not limited to, nor limited by, the material world—Creative Visualization enables humans to reach beyond, into the invisible world of Astral and Spiritual Forces.

Some people apply this innate power without actually knowing what they are doing, and achieve great success and happiness; most people, on the other hand, use this same power, again unknowingly, incorrectly and experience bad luck, failure or, at best, an unfulfilled life.

This book changes that. Through a series of easy, step-by-step, progressive exercises, you will learn how to apply your mind to bring desire into realization! Wealth, power, success, happiness ... even psychic powers ... even what we call magickal power and spiritual attainment ... all can be yours. You can easily develop this completely natural power and correctly apply it, for your immediate and practical benefit.

0-87542-183-0, 304 pgs., 5 1/4 x 8, illus., softcover **$7.95**

PSYCHIC POWER
by Charles Cosimano

Although popular in many parts of the world, *radionics* machines have had little application in America, *UNTIL NOW!* Charles Cosimano's book, *Psychic Power*, introduces these machines to America with a new purpose: to increase your psychic powers!

Using the easy, step-by-step instructions, and for less than a $10.00 investment, you can build a machine which will allow you to read the minds of other people, influence their thoughts, communicate with their dreams, and be more successful when you do divinations such as working with Tarot cards or pendulums.

For thousands of years, people have looked for a simple and sure way to increase their psychic abilities. Now, the science of psionics allows you to do just that! This book is practical, fun and an excellent source for those wishing to achieve results with etheric energies.

If you just want a book to read, you will find this a wonderful title to excitingly fill a few hours. But if you can spare a few minutes to actually build and use these devices, you will be able to astound yourself and your friends. We are not talking about guessing which numbers will come up on a pair of dice at a mark slightly above average. With practice, you will be able to choose which numbers will come up more often than not! But don't take our word for it. Read the book, build the devices and find out for yourself.

0-87542-097-4, 224 pgs., mass market, illus.   **$3.95**

PSIONIC POWER
by Charles Cosimano

Psionic Power picks up where Cosimano's previous Llewellyn title, *Psychic Power*, left off. This new book takes a giant leap forward in the technology of psychic power, and introduces the most powerful radionic devices yet devised.

Although written specifically to guide the radionics veteran onward, *Psionic Power* still serves as a complete guide for the beginner. The author's light and witty style makes high-tech psionics easy and inviting, giving everyone the chance to expand natural psychic ability with much less work than is normally required in other schools of psychic training.

You will learn detailed techniques for projecting psychic power and defending against psychic attack. New devices are diagrammed and explained, and the author includes an informative section on the use of magical sigils with psionic devices. This is the best book yet written on psionics—the final frontier of the New Age!

0-87542-096-6, 224 pgs., mass market, illus.   **$3.95**

HYPNOSIS: A POWER PROGRAM FOR SELF-IMPROVEMENT
by William Hewitt

There is no other hypnosis book on the market that has the depth, scope, and explicit detail as does this book. The exact and complete wordings of dozens of hypnosis routines are given. Real case histories and examples are included for a broad spectrum of situations. Precise instructions for achieving self-hypnosis, the alpha state, and theta state are given. There are dozens of hypnotic suggestions given covering virtually any type of situation one might encounter. The book tells how to become a professional hypnotist. It tells how to become expert at self-hypnosis all by yourself without external help. And it even contains a short dissertation going "beyond hypnosis" into the realm of psychic phenomena. There is something of value here for nearly everyone.

This book details exactly how to gain all you want—to enrich your life at every level. No matter how simple or how profound your goals, this book teaches you how to realize them. The book is not magic; it is a powerful key to unlock the magic within each of us.

0-87542-300-0, 192 pgs., 5 1/4 x 8, softcover $6.95

BEYOND HYPNOSIS
by William Hewitt

This book contains a complete system for using hypnosis to enter a beneficial *altered state of consciousness* in order to develop your psychic abilities. Here is a 30-day program (just 10-20 minutes per day) to release your psychic awareness and then hone it to a fine skill through a series of mental exercises that anyone can do!

Beyond Hypnosis lets you make positive changes in your life. You will find yourself doing things that you only dreamed about in the past: out-of-body experiences; including previously secret instructions to easily and safely leave your body. Learn channeling, where you will easily be able to communicate with spiritual, non-physical entities. With skill improvement, you will be able to learn techniques to improve your physical or mental abilities. Speed up your learning and reading abilities and yet retain more of the information you study. A must for students of all kinds!

Beyond Hypnosis shows you how to create your own reality, how to reshape your own life and the lives of others—and ultimately how to reshape the world and beyond what we call this world! This book will introduce you to a beneficial altered state of consciousness which is achieved by using your own natural abilities to control your mind. It is in this state where you will learn to expand your psychic abilities beyond belief!

0-87542-305-1, 224 pgs., 5 1/4 x 8, softcover $7.95

STROKING THE PYTHON
by Diane Stein

This book is a comprehensive course in psychic understanding, and ends women's psychic isolation forever. It contains the theory and explanation of psychic phenomena, women's shared and varied experiences, and how-to material for every woman's growth and psychic development. The reclamation of being psychic is women's reclamation of Goddess—and of their Goddess Being.

That re-claiming of women's psychic abilities and psychic lives is a major issue in Goddess spirituality and in the wholeness of women. Learning that everyone is psychic, learning what the phenomena mean, sharing and understanding others' experiences, and learning how to develop women's own abilities is information women are ready and waiting for in this dawning Age of Aquarius and Age of Women.

In the Greek legends of Troy, Cassandra, daughter of Hecuba, was gifted with prophecy. She gained her gift as a child at Delphi when she stroked the Python's temple becoming a psychic priestess. The Python, Gaea, was the Goddess of oracles and mother/creator of the Earth.

In this book are fascinating accounts of women's psychic experiences. Learn how to develop your own natural psychic abilities through the extensive advice given in *Stroking the Python*.

0-87542-757-X, 384 pgs., 6 x 9, illus. **$12.95**

PSY-TECH SUBLIMINALS
For Unlocking the Power of Your Subconscious Mind

The mind is the key to growth and change. Llewellyn's *Psy-Tech Subliminals* awaken mental reflexes to assist your behavior modification program.

With Llewellyn's *Subliminals*, you perceive positive, behavior-reinforcing messages underneath the calming roll of ocean waves. Included with each tape are the written subliminal messages and instructions for tape use. Careful research developed *Psy-Tech Subliminals*. Four years of success back them. They work.

ASTRAL PROJECTION takes practice. This tape expands your mind and sharpens your astral link.

0-87542-606-5 **$9.95**

CREATIVE VISUALIZATION is getting what you want from life. You hold the ability to succeed.

0-87542-608-5 **$9.95**